Over the years I've consulted with hundreds of pastors who feel stuck. They want to grow their churches, but they feel stuck and don't know where to turn. I can say with confidence, in knowing James Boyd and watching what has transpired at Grow Church, what you have in this book is an indispensable tool to that very end.

The research of "Christianity Today" revealed 85% of what is taught in seminary is never used. That means two-and-a-half years out of three years of study is virtually useless. Often pastors' training helps us theologically but leaves out many of the tools to effectively accomplish what we want: to expand His kingdom. In *How to Grow a Healthy Church* James Boyd shows pastors the essential tools such as vision casting, empowering leadership, structure for success, stewardship, establishing a working culture, and many more vital keys beyond just the weekend. Read this book to help you expand your part of God's kingdom.

RON MCINTOSH

President, Ron McIntosh Ministries

Author of seven books, including The Missing Ingredient.

———————

Over more than twenty-six years, we have had many wonderful men and women of God minister to our church in Medellin, Colombia, but James Boyd made a different type of impact. He never preached. He never took an offering. He just got down into the engine room of our decision-making process, our relationships, our finances, and our lives. He asked the hard questions.

Prior to James's first visit, we were already a growing church focused on healthy relationships, but we did not have healthy systems. Like a grease monkey with a big toolbox from his church and international business experience, James handed us a few tools as if to say, "You'd better use these," and then he walked us through the changes, encouraging us every step of the way. We did as James directed, and our church has since flourished in health, finances, and spirituality.

I often refer to James Boyd as "Solomon in a pickup truck," and say that his book could be titled *Growing a Healthy Church for Dummies*. In it, James breaks up the clumps of confusion and gives clear blueprints any church can follow. It is a "must" for all pastors in training, and for those who think they are trained. I'd love to see this book in all seminaries, but that would be asking them to teach very practical and useful classes.

I once had lunch with a pastor in Central America whose church numbered twenty thousand. I asked him how it felt to pastor such a growing church. The expression on his face turned sour and he said, "It is so, so hard." I asked for the check and decided right there I only wanted to hang out with pastors who love God, their wives, and the ministry. James Boyd is such a man. He is certainly a man with whom you would like to have lunch too. Enjoy this book over several sandwiches.

ANDREW MCMILLAN

Founding Pastor, Communidad Cristiana de Fe (Christian Community of Faith), Medellin, Columbia

Over the past forty years I have served ministries in many ways. I have been a speaker, helper, worker, and giver, but my most frustrating function in the local church was serving on the church board.

Pastors always want to pray about things, which is a nice way of saying, "I don't want to make any decisions." I think it's their way of not admitting lack of knowledge, which seems to be a missing ingredient in the church. Accepting the gift of administration requires a submission to best practices—this statement is, in essence, the content of Pastor James's book.

Proverbs implores us to get wisdom, and above all else get understanding. Today's churches are important business organizations, and they must operate as such. Allow the Holy Spirit to complete the work He has brought to your Christian community by receiving the information in this book. Life will go easier for you if you do.

BERT LINDSAY

Owner, Lindsay Honda, Lindsay Acura,
Lindsay Buick GMC, Columbus, Ohio

I met James Boyd soon after he returned from his first visit to Medellin, Columbia. At that time, he did not yet know the church he helped in Medellin was part of a very large organization, Mission South America, of which I was a founding board member at its inception in the early 1980s. The ministry now has more than sixty churches worldwide.

As I gave James the history of Mission South America, I quickly realized God's gifting of business and ministry in James was exactly what was needed for Mission South America. I contacted our board president, Dr. Joseph Umidi, and told him about James. Shortly after the two men met to discuss the ministry, we offered James the position of Vice-President of Mission South America, which he accepted.

James has since worked with our apostolic team on the ministry's vision, organization, and financial matters. We have experienced firsthand his ability to identify problems and quickly develop solutions that are often overlooked.

The book you now hold in your hands contains many such solutions to common issues churches and ministries face, as well as practical tools and proven processes that will ensure an organization's optimal health and longevity.

People, including pastors and their staffs, don't like changes. But when changes based on God's wisdom and direction are made in love, the results can be astounding.

It has been my pleasure to get to know James Boyd as a pastor and friend. I testify that he is an extremely talented man who has been called to the Christian community at the direction of the Holy Spirit.

BOB CLAY

Chairman, Coastal Equipment, Virginia Beach, Virginia

The title of this book, *How to Grow a Healthy Church,* is certainly appropriate as it is just the thing James and Tracy Boyd have accomplished with Grow Church in Naples, Florida. There is a fresh and friendly culture with a congregation involved in the dynamics of church life. I could probably say it's the only church of its kind that I know.

I highly recommend this book. It will inspire and challenge the reader, as well as be a great tool for pastors and church planters. The consistent, healthy growth of Grow Church certainly displays the credibility of this book.

MARCELA MACMILLAN

Cofounder and President, Federation of Community of Faith Churches Mission South America

Pastor James Boyd has been blessed in the pulpit as well as in private business. With his unique background, he shares experience from the business sector in a very pragmatic manner that will benefit any pastor whose church is struggling.

Not only has Pastor James led a church with less than fifty members to become a megachurch with a multi-million-dollar annual budget, but he has also guided other churches into getting their financials in order. This book could easily have been titled *Everything You Wanted to Know but Weren't Taught in Seminary* because it successfully fills that void.

It will be a key book in every pastor's library.

GREGORY F. PAINE, MD.

Board Member, Grow Church, Naples, Florida

Pastor James Boyd of Grow Church in Naples, Florida, has written a much-needed book, *How to Grow a Healthy Church*, to help pastors navigate budgeting, systems, accountability, culture, and many other topics not covered in most seminary or Bible schools.

I recommend this book and the online website resource to every pastor and church in America who desires to make an impact with the Great Commission in their city.

PAUL LODATO

Christian Television Network & Founder of Florida Pastors Network

James Boyd has been blessed with a unique set of abilities and passions that have made him into a particularly valuable resource for anyone looking to improve their church management. He has the creativity and drive of an entrepreneur, the attention to detail and problem-solving proficiency of an engineer, and the compassion, authenticity, and communication skill of a pastor-teacher.

As you read this book, you will come to understand that church leadership is more complex than you may have realized. And yet, with the strategies and processes laid out within these pages, along with the assured guidance of the Holy Spirit, you too can build or transform your church into a significant force to advance the kingdom of God here on earth.

WARREN KOOI

Treasurer, Grow Church, Naples, Florida
Minister and Trainer, Restoring the
Foundations, Intl., Naples, Florida

My path to Grow Church came through an unusual connection with the founding pastor of a legit megachurch in Medellin, Colombia. I was so intrigued by his glowing report that I began to attend Grow Church while visiting my home in Naples. I was immediately impressed by the operational fluidity of the service. From arrival to departure, a rare combination of efficiency and sensitivity made me feel right at home.

As I became acquainted with Pastors James and Tracy Boyd, I began to fully appreciate how their individual pedigrees have led to the success of Grow Church. James with an impressive business background, forged in part while working as an executive in Japan, and Tracy as a seasoned orator and natural leader.

How to Grow a Healthy Church will help any church of any size navigate the complexities, peculiarities, and idiosyncrasies of development. Leadership, accountability, culture, and stewardship are all pillars of sustainability for any successful institution, and all are eloquently and thoroughly addressed in this book.

I have twice witnessed the quantifiable success of this book. First, with the amazing turn-around of the mega church in Medellin, and then with my own home church in Raleigh, North Carolina, after having connected their leadership team with the executive team at Grow Church. So, enjoy the read and expect to grow!

TROY A. BUDER, M.B.A.

Senior Wealth Management Advisor, Mercer Global Advisors
Founder and President, TABu Filmz, LLC
Disney Executive Producer, Queen of Katwe

As a tenured professor for twenty-seven years and interim Dean of the School of Divinity for two years, I am aware of the curriculum and training most graduates do not receive in seminary but is critical to their calling and success. Pastor James Boyd has closed that gap in this practical and substantive description of budgeting, systems, accountability, culture, and other must-have topics.

The game changer here is that Pastor James has proven the pages of this book in the dynamic story of Grow Church, which I have visited, followed, and studied. In addition, I have consulted with him internationally and watched him bring major shifts in church networks who have demonstrated the cross-cultural effectiveness of this book.

Pastor James has transferred his extraordinary success in the business community into the church and kingdom with biblical foundations and a love for Jesus. This book belongs in the hands of every church leadership team that will not quit on reaching our culture, and in the hands of every Bible school and seminary student who wants to be fully prepared for what he or she will face for the future of the church.

DR. JOSEPH UMIDI

EVP, Regent University

CEO, Lifeforming Leadership Coaching

Founder, Imagination Partners

Former President, Mission South America

Pastor James Boyd expertly explores principles and topics rarely talked about in church, bringing his wealth of business experience to dynamic church leadership. Diving deep into the behind-the-scenes running of a successful church, James shows that without these principles, the body is without a spine, prone to swaying whichever way the wind is blowing. This book gives necessary ingredients to growing a healthy church, from reaching the unchurched and unsaved, to systems and processes that support long-term growth.

As leaders and pastors, we are tempted to think our Bible school training is all we need and that we are the experts. James's revelations, methods, strategy, and approaches towards church growth and establishing healthy cultures have been pivotal for us and the church we lead. We have seen wonderful growth as we have listened, learned, and implemented many of these principles.

If you long to see growth in your church, then this book is for you. We believe you will see phenomenal fruit come as you learn and apply James's principles, partnering with God, who brings the increase for His glory.

DUNCAN & KATE SMITH

Senior Leaders, Catch the Fire Church, Raleigh, North Carolina

How to Grow a Healthy Church is not just another book, but a manual for success in leading the local church. From the first time I met Pastors James and Tracy Boyd and visited Grow Church, I understood there is something special there.

I've been pastoring for forty years, and every time I enter a church, I'm interested in finding out what makes it tick and how the presence of the Lord is experienced. Grow Church has a unique experience that is so comforting, encouraging, and friendly.

There are so many great churches, but there are so few tools for a local pastor to learn from so that they can grow their churches. This book will help you develop the most important concepts that can take your church to another level in the "behind-the-scenes" aspect of church. It presents church systems, strategy, and processes in a simple, bite-size fashion for immediate implementation. You will absolutely find helpful tools that will change the dynamics of your church.

Enjoy this book and get ready to take some notes for your personal application in church leadership.

RAMIRO PEÑA

Pastor, Christ the King Church, Waco, Texas
CEO, Ramiro Peña Ministries

HOW TO GROW A HEALTHY CHURCH

[the stuff they don't teach at seminary]

HOW TO GROW A HEALTHY CHURCH

[the stuff they don't teach at seminary]

JAMES BOYD

How to Grow a Healthy Church
[the stuff they don't teach at seminary]

Published by Influential Productions
Bonita Springs, Florida

Editorial, design and production: Vision Book Producers, Edmond, Oklahoma: visionbookproducers.com

Back cover and bio portrait photography: Pure Fotografica, Bonita Springs, Florida: purefotografica.com

This book is dedicated to my wife, Tracy, without whom it would have been impossible to grow a healthy church.

Many say it takes two to tango, and that is the case here. Tracy and I have put countless hours into pastoring, mentoring, and building healthy church systems to fulfill the calling God has placed on our lives. I would pick no other teammate for this assignment.

Tracy's wisdom and revelation into the things of God has been not only inspiring, but also motivating through the tough times of building a church. There is no greater resource on the planet for a guy like me than a supportive, encouraging, and God-honoring wife who continues to pour out grace when others don't. I can truly say this book would not be possible without Tracy and her dedication to me and the ministry.

I love you, Tracy—the best years are still ahead!

CONTENTS

According to one research organization, the United States has more than 1,500 megachurches with weekly attendance numbering anywhere from 2,000 to 44,000 people. However, the greatest percentage of churches in the United States have a weekly attendance of less than 100 people and do not experience any measurable growth in those numbers. Low numbers and lack of growth have nothing to do with the pastor's knowledge of the Bible; rather, the condition oftentimes stems from his or her inability to apply the Bible to the business side of the church.

As both a businessman and a pastor, I've come to understand that if we do not steward the churches we are called to lead in a God-honoring way, we will not experience His blessings to the fullest. Churches that do not experience consistent growth are not representative of the New Testament church, of which the Bible says, *And the Lord added to the church daily those who were being saved* (Acts 2:47). The fledgling church described in the book of Acts needed everything from great preaching to miracles and wonders to thrive.

But they also needed organization.

Acts, chapter 6, describes how the twelve initially set up the practical (or business) side of the growing ministry, saying, *"Therefore, brethren, seek out from among you seven men of good reputation, full of the Holy Spirit and wisdom, whom we may appoint over this business"* (verse 3). A powerful anointing comes upon any church that chooses to step into the gift of administration and creates simple processes and systems that allow people to engage in the local body of Christ.

Most churches do not spend the appropriate time needed to build their operational teams and systems; therefore, they usually cap at a certain size and never grow past it. Though this is always the pastor's problem, it is usually not his or her fault. Pastors are not trained in the business aspect of running a church, a topic not addressed in seminaries and Bible colleges that generally focus solely on theology. It is, of course, vital to be grounded in theology, but it is equally important to be grounded in the processes and systems of ministry, without which there will be no healthy growth.

Over the years I've had countless conversations with pastors concerning the business side of their churches as it pertains to processes, administration, and finances. One of the initial questions I always ask is, "How do you budget?" I'm no longer surprised to learn that a pastor does not budget. Some genuinely don't know the meaning of the word, some feel that budgeting hinders them from following God, and others say that budgeting is unnecessary for an institution led by God.

I can appreciate the sentiment about following God when it comes to leading a church; however, the Bible is filled with examples of how God guides *people* to do His work. The way I see it,

God leads the local church by collaborating with a willing vessel. God had much to say about stewardship, which He spoke through those who penned the Bible for Him. If He truly uses people to accomplish His purposes (and He does), then our willingness to plan and strategize our ministries in advance is the greatest key to seeing God move in enormous ways.

One practice we implemented early on at the church we lead was to measure every process within to assess its usefulness. We of course kept track of our giving, and we also kept track of the number of salvations, baptisms, and attendees in our discipleship program. We measured everything of value to us, which enabled us to see where we had opportunity to make necessary changes.

As believers, we honor God when we make things that are important to Him important to us. Every soul matters to God and, as such, should matter to us. In our local church body, we didn't want to chase people away from God because our systems or procedures were too complicated or difficult to follow. Even today, we know our systems need to evolve until the day Jesus returns, and for this reason we continue to improve the business side of the church in ways that always honor God.

I've often heard people say that the church is not a business, but I disagree. I believe the church is God's business, and He's serious about it. The church should be run with the same respect a business is run; I say this as a business owner and entrepreneur. My wife, Tracy, and I have been called to the bivocational ministry, and God has blessed us in our business, enabling us to be one of the biggest givers to our church as we lead it. We made an agreement with God that if He runs our business, we'll run His. This arrangement has worked out well for us.

At God's direction and with His partnership, Tracy and I have built a large ministry (in our perspective) that can support us and our family, but we've decided not to let it. Ours is certainly a different approach to ministry than that of most pastors, but it's allowed us to view the behind-the-scenes aspect of the local church as a business that needs solid systems, processes, and accountability. And it is these systems, processes, and account-ability measures that I will now share with you.

Perhaps you are a church pastor or ministry leader who is not experiencing the kind of growth you would like to see. As I said, though the issue may not be your fault, it is nonetheless yours to deal with. Or you may be a young pastor about to step out in faith and answer God's call to plant a church. Regardless of where you're located on your ministry path, I believe the practical infor-mation and insights laid out in this book will serve as the effective arsenal of tools you need to grow a healthy church or ministry.

PART ONE

A SURE FOUNDATION

For we are all fellow workers; you are God's field, you are God's building. According to the grace of God which was given to me, as a wise master builder I have laid the foundation, and another builds on it. But let each one take heed how he builds on it. For no other foundation can anyone lay than that which is laid, which is Jesus Christ.

1 CORINTHIANS 3:9–11

GROW CHURCH TODAY: A PICTURE OF HEALTH

In January 2017 my wife, Tracy, and I were actively engaged in our long-established practice of putting together our annual prayer list, which we would subsequently pray over every day throughout the year. Our lists invariably included a good number of thoroughly audacious goals, things we could never complete on our own. These goals always required manifestations of God's miracle-working power. We had long ago come to believe that God liked us to take this approach in believing Him for things far beyond our ability to accomplish.

One such audacious goal for 2017 was that Grow Church, the church we pastor in Naples, Florida, would be debt-free by the end of the year; that goal was number one on our prayer list. We then found promises in the Bible that confirmed a debt-free church was the will of God for us. We read about God's people being debt-free, about their being the lender and not the borrower according to Deuteronomy 28:12: *The LORD will open to you His good treasure, the heavens, to give the rain to your land in its season, and to bless all the work of your hand. You shall lend to many nations, but you shall not borrow.* So we wrote that promise next to our prayer request, and then every morning we read it, meditated on it, and declared that Grow Church would be a debt-free church by the end of 2017.

But within sixty days we had another matter to pray about: our expanding church family had already outgrown two previous buildings, and at the rate of our current exponential growth, we would soon require yet another, even larger, building. At that point what we needed most was God's wisdom and direction, which became the focus of our prayers.

Tracy and I were confident in our request for wisdom, for the Bible says, *If any of you lacks wisdom, let him ask of God, who gives to all liberally and without reproach, and it will be given to him* (James 1:5). Being debt-free by the end of the year *and* having a facility large enough for our growing congregation was far beyond our ability; it would take God's intervention. Though in the natural achieving our goal seemed impossible, we continued to pray.

Around July of 2017 a gentleman we knew came to us and said, "Pastors James and Tracy, I was just at another church not far from here and it seems that they could use some financial help. I know Grow Church has helped other churches in this way, and I wonder if you'd consider helping them." We said we would look into the matter.

The following Monday morning Tracy and I got in our vehicle and went to locate the church with the intention of merely looking at the facility. As it turned out, the pastor was in his office that day, and we had the opportunity to sit down and talk with him. He openly shared the church's financial status and the challenges they faced in trying to find a way to make some needed repairs to the building. Bottom line was, his was a small congregation struggling to maintain a large building, and we were a growing congregation bursting at the proverbial seams in a small building.

Our congregation also prayed with us about the new facility and being debt free.

Sensing God's presence in our impromptu meeting with the pastor, and without first discussing the matter with my wife, I said, "Pastor, would you be open to a church swap?" Tracy later told me that she thought the pastor's response would be to throw us out of his office. But he didn't throw us out—as a matter of fact he said yes to the possibility of an exchange—so when we left his office that day, we had the sense that God was moving.

We met with our board of trustees to discuss the possibility of a church swap and the positive logistic impact it could have on both congregations; however, doing so would also impact Grow Church's finances, and not in a positive way. Because the larger church building needed some substantial repairs, getting into it would literally double our current debt.

Despite the obvious drawbacks to the idea of a church swap, Tracy and I felt the Lord was leading us to move forward, so every morning we continued to pray, meditate, and declare, "In the name of Jesus, we believe according to the promises in the

Word of God that Grow Church will be debt-free by the end of the year!" Our congregation also prayed with us about the new facility and being debt-free.

A couple of months later, following the Sunday morning service, a couple who lives in Naples part time told me and Tracy that they might be able to help Grow Church get into the larger building, and asked if they could meet with us. We scheduled a meeting with them later that day at a local coffee shop.

The first thing the man said when the four of us sat down at the shop was, "Pastors James and Tracy, when we talked to you this morning, my wife and I felt God was directing us to give you $100,000 to help you get into your new church facility." I thought, *That's God!* Then with his next breath he said, "But we've reconsidered and no longer believe that's what we are to do." My next thought was, *No, that's not God. You need to help us with that $100,000!* The man continued, "My wife and I were talking as we drove to the coffee shop to meet you, and we both feel that we've heard from the Lord. We now believe that we're supposed to do the deal."

I wasn't sure I knew what "do the deal" meant, but my mind was spinning because it sounded to me like those words could mean *cover the entire cost of the building*. As it turned out, that's exactly what they meant.

That one couple who heard from the Lord to "do the deal" for Grow Church gave $3.5 million to cover the entire loan amount required to purchase the property. We were debt-free when we moved into our new building.

WITH GOD, NOTHING IS IMPOSSIBLE

"Behold, I am the LORD, the God of all flesh. Is there anything too hard for Me?" (JEREMIAH 32:27).

Our debt-free status didn't last long. After moving into the new building, we had a setback when Hurricane Irma ripped through south Florida during the afternoon of September 10, flooding coastal cities, blowing down trees, and inflicting damage to homes, buildings, and roofs, including ours. Our insurance experts told us it was highly unlikely we'd get a large enough payout to replace the roof and cover damages, which meant we'd have to incur some debt. But we were not dissuaded. We continued to stand on God's Word, believing for a structurally sound and debt-free church by the end of 2017, for the Bible makes this promise: *You shall also decide and decree a thing, and it shall be established for you; and the light [of God's favor] shall shine upon your ways* (Job 22:28 AMPC). The Bible also says, *"For with God nothing will be impossible"* (Luke 1:37).

Against all natural odds, we received a *full* insurance payout, and by the end of December 2017—just as we'd prayed, believed, and decreed—not only was Grow Church totally debt-free, but after completing repairs of the hurricane damage, the value of the church and property had increased to $7.4 million. We had stood on the Word of God in faith, and because of our obedience to proclaim God's promises over Grow Church, we experienced the fulfillment of those promises.

I particularly like to read Ephesians 3:20 in the Amplified Bible, Classic Edition, which says, *Now to Him Who, by (in consequence of) the [action of His] power that is at work within us, is able to [carry out His purpose and] do superabundantly, far over and above all that we[dare] ask or think [infinitely beyond our highest prayers, desires, thoughts, hopes, or dreams].* Not only did God answer the audacious prayer Tracy and I prayed at the beginning of the year, that Grow Church would be debt-free, but He went far beyond all we could ask or think and *more than doubled* the value of our property.

Today Grow Church is a vibrant, healthy, and growing congregation that serves southwest Florida from its two locations in Naples, with three more locations anticipated in the coming three to five years. We have over one hundred small home groups, named Grow Groups, scattered throughout Naples and the neighboring Gulf Coast communities of Fort Myers, Estero, Bonita Springs, the Isles of Capri, and Marco Island.

Not only is Grow Church spiritually healthy, but it is also financially healthy. Whereas the national average for church giving is around 3 percent of annual income, Grow Church has given a little over 21 percent of the church's income, which, at the time of this writing, was over $600,000 last year. Because we are deliberate in our financial planning and in stewarding God's money well, we are not only able to impact our own community, but our outreach extends to the nation and the world as well.

Though Naples is situated in Collier County where, according to Forbes.com, Americans with money continue to move on a steady basis, there is still great need in some nearby communities. For instance, only thirty minutes from Naples is an impoverished small town in which the poverty rate is 43.4 percent—not surprising since Jesus said, *"The poor you will always have with you"*

(Matthew 26:11 NIV). The people in this community are frequent recipients of our monthly "serve events." We also have an annual, expanded serve event that targets seven to ten groups at one time as we send out literally hundreds of people in a single day to help those in need.

One small denominational church that didn't have the funds to renovate their facility was thrilled when we gave them a check to cover the costs and sent volunteers to help with the repairs. We also partner with multiple organizations that organize local outreaches to areas of need within the foster-care system, schools, hospitals, and the homeless community.

On a national level we partner with the Association of Related Churches (ARC) both in church planting and in assisting a plethora of organizations, including fiscally responsible startup churches.

Grow Church's international influence is perhaps strongest in South America, where we've built a feeding center in Costa Rica, sent missionaries to Colombia, and helped rescue women from the sex-trafficking industry and then aid them in transitioning to jobs in other industries. We also have a missionary presence in quite a few other nations, as well as providing continual support to leadership and evangelistic efforts in Israel, because we believe what the Bible says: *And so all Israel will be saved* (Romans 11:26).

Jesus said, *"Go into all the world and preach the gospel to every creature"* (Mark 16:15), and that's exactly what we are doing.

CALLED TO BIVOCATIONAL MINISTRY

For God's gifts and His call are irrevocable. [*He never*
withdraws them when once they are given, and He does not
change His mind about those to whom He gives His grace
or to whom He sends His call] (ROMANS 11:29 AMPC).

Though Grow Church is a picture of health in all areas, it wasn't
always so. In 2011 Tracy and I lived in Michigan, where we were
busy raising our three young daughters, growing our real-estate
investing-and-management companies, and serving in leadership
capacities at our local church. In that local body I served as technical director and youth-and-young-adult pastor, and she served
as associate pastor, worship leader, and children's pastor.

I had grown up in a Christian home and served many days
every week in the local church with my family. Tracy had grown up
in a break-off of the Mormon church but had become a Christian
after experiencing a miraculous healing from God. We had both
served in our individual local churches for many years (minus the
nine-year road trip I took from my faith in my late teens and early
twenties, which I won't elaborate on in this book).

When Tracy and I married, we both knew God had called us to
what we refer to as "bivocational ministry," meaning we were to
be businesspeople as well as pastors. Much credit goes to Tracy's
mom, a devoted Christian, whose own profound calling was, at
the time, managing business and planting churches. In creating
self-sustaining business entities that generated passive income,

Tracy and I had the freedom to spend much of our time working within our local church and funding its initiatives.

Now a word about bivocational ministry: If you're not called by God to do it, *don't do it.* Businesses and churches in the process of expanding generate a lot of pressure that can crush anyone who does not operate under God's direction and grace. One of the Bible verses God gave Tracy and me when He called us into bivocational ministry was 2 Corinthians 9:8: *And God is able to make all grace abound toward you, that you, always having all sufficiency in all things, may have an abundance for every good work.* When God calls anyone to any level of ministry, that calling always comes with the strength and ability to handle it.

So in 2011 Tracy and I had answered the call to bivocational ministry, and God had honored our obedience. What we didn't know was that our obedience would lead us far beyond the borders of our home state of Michigan and the small church we served there. That part of our journey started in July of that same year when Tracy's mother, Sarah, traveled to Naples, Florida, with the intention of purchasing a winter home. While in Naples, her real estate agent introduced her to someone whose church was floundering following a recent split in its leadership.

Sarah called us and asked if we would come to Naples to help the congregation, and we said yes. Our partnership in Michigan had just closed a big business deal, so Tracy and I figured we'd fly the 1,300 miles to Naples, write a check, and then return home and go on with our lives. After we arrived in southwest Florida and took some time to drive around the area, we understood why Naples was advertised as "The Jewel of the Paradise Coast."

Though small in comparison to most cities, Naples's white-sand beaches, wild islands, world-class shopping and dining, warm winter temperatures, and generally laid-back atmosphere make it a favorite Gulf Coast destination for people from all over the world. Little wonder my mother-in-law wanted to spend her winters there.

When Tracy and I met with the members of the church's board, we discovered the situation was worse than we'd imagined. Without pastoral leadership, the congregation had plummeted to a total of fifty people, including children and youth, and the church was in the red financially. We assessed they were about one week away from closing their doors, yet we sensed something special about the board members and the small group of believers struggling to survive without a pastor. By the end of our meeting, the board viewed us as a God-sent lifeline, and they asked if we would consider taking over the church. We left with our promise to pray about the matter and get back to them quickly with our answer.

Within a week God had spoken clearly to both Tracy and me: the answer was *yes* to the church in Naples. We immediately began taking turns flying from Michigan to Florida weekly to triage the church and preach each Sunday so that one of us would always be home with our children. But then God asked us this question: "Are you willing to *move* to Naples?" We didn't have to give the matter a second thought, for we'd already fallen in love with the church and the people. Once we said yes to God, things happened quickly, and within ninety days of receiving the initial call from Tracy's mother, we were Florida residents.

The first question Tracy and I asked ourselves after taking the helm of the church was whether we could create a church we would want to attend—even if we weren't leading it—and if so, what would it look like? We loved our church in Michigan, but throughout the years we'd served there, we'd seen things that we would have changed had we been leading it. Now we had the opportunity to implement the policies and procedures—including a healthy dose of sound business practices—we believed would establish a solid foundation on which the little church could grow.

FIRST THINGS FIRST

"Whom will he teach knowledge? And whom will he make to understand the message? ... For precept must be upon precept, precept upon precept, line upon line, line upon line, here a little, there a little" (ISAIAH 28:9–10).

Once in Naples, our first order of business was to stabilize the church, both financially and spiritually. Our businesses supported our family of five and allowed us to underwrite some of the church's needs in that initial season while we worked with God to resuscitate the church.

We had a small, faithful group of people committed to their church's survival, so we started the stabilization process with the board, requesting of them that, moving forward, they allow us to designate 10 percent of the church's income to giving. Doing so was, at first, a hard pill to swallow for the board members, some of whom had never been taught the biblical principle of tithing. Tracy and I patiently taught them what the Bible has to say about the matter and shared our own personal account of the connection between our tithing and God's blessing in our lives. In so doing, we cited Malachi 3:10 as God's promise to *all* who tithe: *"Bring all the tithes into the storehouse, that there may be food in My house, and try Me now in this," says the LORD of hosts, "If I will not open for you the windows of heaven and pour out for you such a blessing that there will not be room enough to receive it."* Once the board members took ownership of the Bible truth that tithing was the key that opened the door to God's blessings, we had their enthusiastic support.

> *Our focus at Grow Church was, and is, always on the unsaved and the unchurched; we've learned that when we do this, growth happens organically.*

I understand tithing can be a complicated theological viewpoint; therefore, to keep the topic simple in this writing, let's look at it this way:If you're not comfortable with the term *tithing* from a church perspective, because scripture shows that the church is the receiver of the tithe, just think about tithing as *being generous*. Since we cannot out-give God, this generosity positions the church to support the poor, the widow, and the orphan, as well as many other faith-based initiatives, as the Bible directs.

Our next step was to infuse faith into our congregation. After teaching them about tithing, we took everyone through one of the Bible courses we had taught at our church in Michigan. Based on Kenneth E. Hagin's classic book *The Believer's Authority*, the course teaches believers about the powerful authority God has given us on earth and how to exercise that authority by using our God-given weapons of spiritual warfare against the power of the devil. In just a short time, both the board and congregation were on the same page with us.

Though we had inherited a good core group of people that we could train as leaders, the Lord's instruction to me and Tracy was to move forward as if we were establishing a start-up church. We'd never started a church as the primary leaders before, and we knew we'd have to rely heavily on the Lord for His direction; we were ready to take our prayer life to a new level as we moved forward in the uncharted waters before us.

Tracy and I had done a lot of talking about what was important to us in a church, and at the top of our list was that it be focused on the unsaved and unchurched. We envisioned a church where Sunday services were intentionally structured for people to experience God because we knew that those who truly sought to change their lives often visited at that time. We wanted every person in attendance to have a cordial invitation to meet Jesus.

We were, of course, aware that many vibrant churches oftentimes experience significant increase through "transfer growth," which means people come from other churches. The reasons individuals change churches are varied: God may call some to change churches to advance their spiritual growth or because their unique gifts and talents are needed there, while others choose to change churches because they've been hurt. Certainly, nobody intends to hurt another believer, but hurts do happen—we see it all the time. Nevertheless, our focus at Grow Church was, and is, always on the unsaved and the unchurched; we've learned that when we do this, growth happens organically.

SCHOOLED IN THE WORLD, SCHOOLED IN THE WORD

So Moses was educated in all the wisdom and culture of the Egyptians, and he was mighty (powerful) in his speech and deeds (ACTS 7:22 AMPC).

Though Moses was the man chosen by God to perform miracles as he led God's people out of slavery in Egypt, he was also well educated in matters of practical wisdom. God had perfectly equipped him to handle both the spiritual and natural aspects of leading some two million people out of captivity to live for forty years in the Sinai desert.

Whether God calls an individual as the pastor of a church or the leader of a ministry, accomplishing the call with success requires both schooling in the world and schooling in the Word. In my theological schooling I received a solid foundation of Bible truths and principles that grew my faith immensely, but there was something missing in my preparation for ministry: my training lacked education in business, budgeting, and the necessary processes required to run a church.

Most pastors come out of seminary with enough books on spiritual matters to fill a wall of shelves but none that help them lead the church from a business perspective. Seminary and Bible school graduates are left to figure out these practical matters on their own. Thankfully, I was already an experienced businessman prior to my theological training.

Church is ministry, but it's also *business*. Pastors and leaders who do not have the practical training they need to run a church will likely face a long, hard road before them. Some have said, "Well, Pastor James, aren't churches supposed to be nonprofit organizations?" Yes, they are. However, a church requires money so that it can grow and profit *people*. If pastors and leaders can't budget for the future, how will they have the funds they need to do what God calls them to do, when He calls them to do it? They will always be one step behind God, continually frustrated by the stories of other churches who get the bigger building or the new location.

I've seen what God can do when He imparts business wisdom into the local church, and I am convinced that God intends pastors and ministry leaders to steward His resources in a way that we can accomplish what He calls us to do, when He calls us to do it.

Now I want to speak directly to you. Perhaps you feel spiritually or financially "stuck" in your church or ministry, or there may be some dreams you haven't reached for because they seem impossible. When Tracy and I make our annual prayer lists, the things we ask for are daring in that they can't be accomplished without a miracle from God. I want to encourage you to give yourself the opportunity to experience a miracle, to give God an opportunity to do a miracle in your life.

I particularly like Acts 10:34 in The Passion Translation: *Peter said, "Now I know for certain that God doesn't show favoritism with people but treats everyone on the same basis."* In other words, what

God has done for me and Tracy—and for Grow Church—He will most certainly do for you and your church or ministry as well. But growing a healthy church doesn't just happen; it takes strategy, budgeting, implementation, execution, leadership, understanding, and business savvy. When you take the time to educate yourself in these practical matters, and then prepare well, according to the principles established in the Word of God, He will open the doors of heaven and pour out a blessing you cannot contain (see Malachi 3:9–10).

I've written this book as a tool to help you get from where you are to where you want to be as you pursue your dreams and passion to grow your church or ministry beyond all that you can think or ask. If you are willing to apply yourself to getting wisdom, knowledge, and understanding—both spiritual and practical—then, according to Ephesians 3:20, you will see God do immeasurably more than you ask or imagine, according to the power that is at work within you.

Now let's get to work.

CHAPTER ONE REVIEW:

1. Audacious goals call for God to intervene, because they are bigger than what we can accomplish in our own human strength.

   » **CHALLENGE:** Create some audacious goals beyond what you could do without God's intervention. Share these goals with your staff and encourage them to hold the goals up in prayer along with you. Nothing is more powerful than the prayer of agreement between group members heading in the same direction.

2. Making room for excessive giving shows God that we can be trusted with what He gives us, even if it's a small start.

   » **CHALLENGE:** Be deliberate in your financial planning by establishing a giving goal larger than last year's total giving. Give God something to work with and your staff something to pray toward.

3. Budgets help ministries gain control of their finances so that they can be ready to do what God calls them to do, when He calls them to do it.

   » **CHALLENGE:** Create an annual budget (if you don't already have one). Share it with your staff members so that they understand the boundaries they are working with.

4. Business knowledge in church is vital for the healthy growth of your church.

   » **CHALLENGE:** Find some helpful podcasts, books, coaching, or conferences to attend this year to help you see the church from the executive perspective.

_____

_____

_____

_____

A SUPERNATURAL FOUNDATION: PRAYER, GENEROSITY, AND MARGIN

"A successful man is one who can lay a firm foundation
with the bricks others have thrown at him."

—DAVID BRINKLEY

"Laying a solid foundation for your business will provide
you with a road map to follow as you build your business."

—JEANNE A. ESTES

"A grateful heart is a beginning of greatness. It is
an expression of humility. It is a foundation for the
development of such virtues as prayer, faith, courage,
contentment, happiness, love, and well-being."

—JAMES E. FAUST

I am often asked questions that can be summed up like this: "Pastor James, to what do you attribute the success of Grow Church and its amazing outreach to your city, your state, the nation, and the world?" My answer is that Tracy and I laid a deliberate supernatural foundation consisting of these three elements: prayer, generosity, and margin.

When people hear my answer, most of them look at me like I have a frog on my forehead. They understand the biblical principles of prayer and generosity, but ... *margin?* You may be thinking, *Really? Where's that in the Bible?* Just be patient, keep reading, and we'll let the Bible show us how margin is the natural outcome of prayer and generosity.

PRAYER

"Again I say to you that if two of you agree on earth concerning anything that they ask, it will be done for them by My Father in heaven. For where two or three are gathered in My name, I am there in the midst of them" (MATTHEW 18:20).

Nothing in this life changes or grows without prayer. Some may say, "God is sovereign, and He can do anything He wants to do." Yes, He can, but He *chooses* to work in partnership with mankind to see His plans and purposes fulfilled in the earth.

The Word of God has this to say about prayer: *The effective, fervent prayer of a righteous man avails much. Elijah was a man with a nature like ours, and he prayed earnestly that it would not rain; and it did not rain on the land for three years and six months. And he prayed again, and the heaven gave rain, and the earth produced its fruit* (James 5:16–18). This portion of scripture is a reference to the story in 1 Kings that happened during a time of drought and famine in the land:

> And it came to pass after many days that the word of the LORD came to Elijah, in the third year, saying, "Go, present yourself to Ahab, and I will send rain on the earth."
>
> And Elijah went up to the top of Carmel; then he bowed down on the ground, and put his face between his knees, and he said to his servant, "Go up now, look toward the sea."
>
> So he went up and looked and said, "There is nothing." And seven times [Elijah] said, "Go again."
>
> Then it came to pass the seventh time, that he said, "There is a cloud, as small as a man's hand, rising out of the sea!" So he said, "Go up, say to Ahab, 'Prepare your chariot, and go down before the rain stops you.'"
>
> Now it happened in the meantime that the sky became black with clouds and wind, and there was a heavy rain (1 KINGS 18:1, 42–45)

God's Word to Elijah was clear, "I will send rain on the earth," yet Elijah bowed to the ground and prayed seven times before the rain manifested. God's plans don't "just happen" on earth; they come as the result of prayer. We see this principle demonstrated in the New Testament as well. For instance, healing belongs to all who have made Jesus Lord and Savior, yet it manifests through prayer: *Is anyone among you suffering? Let him pray ... Is anyone among you sick? Let him call for the elders of the church, and let them pray over him ... and the prayer of faith will save the sick, and the Lord will raise him up* (James 5:13–15).

Nothing happens without prayer. Grow Church would not exist if it weren't for prayer. This is not simply a statement we make; it's the absolute truth. Prayer is our number one priority, which we demonstrate in a multitude of ways, of which the following four are the most significant.

- **INTERCESSION TEAM:** This group of men and women pray together every Saturday for our weekend services and throughout the week for the prayer-request forms submitted by our church family. Additionally, the team members gather in a prayer room in shifts during each of our weekend services to ensure our pastors, staff, volunteers, and congregation are covered in live prayer.

- **PRAYER TEAM:** Members of this team are available at the end of every service to meet with those in need of personal prayer. We always highlight the prayer team for attendees and encourage them with the words of Jesus: *"And these signs will follow those who believe: In My name they will cast out demons; they will speak with new tongues; they will take up serpents; and if they drink anything deadly, it will by no means hurt them; they will lay hands on the sick, and they will recover"* (Mark 16:17–18).

- **TWENTY-ONE DAYS OF PRAYER AND FASTING:** This event is exactly what its name suggests. Twice each year our Grow family meets daily at seven o'clock in the morning—either in person at the church or via livestream—for an hour of corporate prayer, which remains available online for the subsequent twenty-three hours until the next meeting. A staff member leads each prayer session and demonstrates to those in attendance how to pray powerful, Bible-based prayers, most of which are based on the Lord's Prayer from Matthew 6. Additionally, many members throughout the area open their homes each evening at seven o'clock for those who cannot attend the morning sessions and still desire an in-person, group prayer meeting.

- **THE PRAYER OF SALVATION:** We pray the prayer of salvation during every weekend service because we believe that doing so gives the greatest opportunity for people to meet Jesus. We understand that most first-time visitors choose to come to a Sunday service; therefore, our weekend services are referred to in-house as "serve the salvation" services. We take this prayer seriously, because it is a new believer's first step in his or her walk with the Lord.

These are just a few examples of how we esteem prayer. Without prayer, Grow Church would not be the healthy church it is today.

GENEROSITY

*"Give, and it will be given to you: good measure, pressed
down, shaken together, and running over will be put
into your bosom. For with the same measure that you
use, it will be measured back to you"* (LUKE 6:38).

We attribute our generosity as the second reason we have a
healthy church. Grow Church gives away 10 percent of our annual
budget, paid out in monthly increments. Statistics show that most
churches across the nation give only 3 percent annually. Then
twice each year we evaluate the difference between our income
and budget. Because of the way we budget, our income is always
higher than projected, so we adjust our giving accordingly, which
always means *more* giving.

There are numerous ways we express our generosity through
giving. Our monthly *serve events* are a great way for our Grow
family to be involved in meeting specific needs in our community,
which Grow Church also backs with funding. The Bible says, *He
who has a generous eye will be blessed, for he gives bread to the poor*
(Proverbs 22:9). Several times each year we provide *giving bags* for
our church family to take home and fill with specific items, which
are then distributed to those in need in our area. Each Christmas
we sponsor a *giving tree* for less fortunate families in our own
church as well as in our community.

Our benevolence budget is managed by a committee that
oversees funding for those in need; however, we don't simply give
people money and then move on. We help them break free from

the cycle of poverty by working with them to set up a personal budget and take charge of their finances.

Grow Church's generosity is a topic that Tracy and I deliberately and frequently talk about from the pulpit. We learned from the book *Building a Story Brand* by Donald Miller that the people in our church family are the heroes, not Grow Church or its staff. We celebrate our church family for *their* generosity; the church is just the means through which their generosity is distributed to our community. We purpose to take the time in a Sunday service to tell our Grow family exactly what they sponsored and the results that were achieved, and then we thank our church family for their generosity in making it happen.

It's unthinkable that God would be stingy in helping people or other churches, so neither are we.

One of our most commented-on expressions of generosity is the way we stock our restrooms. We consider any unexpected need someone might have when away from home and then supply each restroom with products to meet those needs. We found our well-stocked restrooms to be a selling point for first-time visitors. Go figure.

We express our generosity in ways both small and large, from always providing free coffee any time the doors are open to allowing other churches access to our systems, processes, procedures, and documentation (always within legal parameters). Grow Church is not our church, it's God's church. It's unthinkable that God would be stingy in helping people or other churches, so neither are we.

Generosity is not something we talk about; it is something we represent. When it comes to generosity, our viewpoint is this: Don't say it; do it. Don't act like the Church; *be* the Church—the body of Christ—that Jesus talked about and described as His bride, the hope of the world.

MARGIN

> *And God is able to make all grace (every favor and earthy blessing) come to you in abundance, so that you may always and under all circumstances and whatever the need be self-sufficient [possessing enough to require no aid or support and furnished in abundance for every good work and charitable donation]* (2 CORINTHIANS 9:8 AMPC).

As I said at the beginning of this chapter, margin is the natural outcome of prayer and generosity. Though our modern-day English word *margin* is not found in the Bible, the concept of setting aside money or provision is a sound biblical principle:

- *On the first day of every week each one of you is to put aside and save* (1 Corinthians 16:2).

- *For children are not responsible to save up for their parents, but parents for their children* (2 Corinthians 12:14).

- *A good man leaves an inheritance to his children's children* (Proverbs 13:22).

- *The ransom of a man's life is his wealth* (Proverbs 13:8).

- *She considers a field and buys it; from her earnings she plans a vineyard* (Proverbs 31:16).

Now let's look at the familiar story of Elisha and the prophet's widow through the lens of margin:

A certain woman of the wives of the sons of the prophets cried out to Elisha, saying, "Your servant my husband is dead, and you know that your servant feared the LORD. And the creditor is coming to take my two sons to be his slaves."

So Elisha said to her, "What shall I do for you? Tell me, what do you have in the house?" And she said, "Your maidservant has nothing in the house but a jar of oil."

Then he said, "Go, borrow vessels from everywhere, from all your neighbors—empty vessels; do not gather just a few. And when you have come in, you shall shut the door behind you and your sons; then pour into all those vessels, and set aside the full ones."

So she went from him and shut the door behind her and her sons, who brought the vessels to her; and she poured it out. Now it came to pass, when the vessels were full, that she said to her son, "Bring me another vessel."

And he said to her, "There is not another vessel." So the oil ceased. Then she came and told the man of God. And he said, "Go, sell the oil and pay your debt; and you and your sons live on the rest" (2 Kings 4:1–7).

Though the widow didn't know it, that jar of oil was her *margin*. Notice Elisha didn't tell her to sow her jar of oil as a seed; rather, he instructed her to do the work necessary to prepare for God's intervention in her situation and the miracle coming her way. Her part was to gather all the empty vessels she could find (creating margin), and God's part was to fill them. He multiplied her margin, not only meeting her immediate need, but also leaving her with enough savings for the future.

Saving money demonstrates good stewardship of the resources God gives us and allows us to be prepared for the future. God demonstrates this principle in nature: *There are four things which are little on earth, but they are exceedingly wise: The ants are a people not strong, yet they prepare their food in the summer* (Proverbs 30:24–25).

If we don't plan for the future and save, we can easily go into debt, a situation the Bible describes this way: *The rich rules over the poor, and the borrower is servant to the lender* (Proverbs 22:7). We know going into debt is not what God wants for His people, because Moses spoke to the generation destined to possess the Promised Land and said, *"For the LORD your God will bless you just as He promised you; you shall lend to many nations, but you shall not borrow; you shall reign over many nations, but they shall not reign over you"* (Deuteronomy 15:6).

I refer to margin most any time I talk about business and church. Sadly, margin is a foreign term to most of the church world, though it's common practice in the business world.

We stand on our faith, proving it by our works of creating margin, building it into our budgets, and making room for God to step in and perform His miracle.

Business owners are keenly aware of margin, the difference between their income and expenses measured as a percentage. Margin is a trustworthy indicator of long-term viability because margin accounts for unexpected developments that could cut into a business's profits. Margin is what keeps businesses safe and their budgets healthy.

Margin is also what keeps churches safe and their budgets healthy. Simply stated, *margin enables churches and pastors to do what God calls them to do, when He calls them to do it.*

From my unique perspective as both a pastor and business-man, the concept of margin is less important in the church world than in the business world. The primary reason for this disparity is that the business world is built on actual income and expense models that dictate outcomes, whereas the church is built primarily on faith. Most certainly, faith is the foundation on which any God-ordained endeavor should be built, for the Bible says, *Now faith is the substance of things hoped for, the evidence of things not seen* (Hebrews 11:1). But seminaries all over the planet are shortsighted when they teach that *all* one needs is faith. I believe in the kind of faith that supersedes our ability to plan—Tracy and I know first-hand that bold, audacious faith works—but the Bible also says, *For as the body without the spirit is dead, so faith without works is dead* (James 2:26). In other words, our works prove our faith.

I personally consider diligence a work that proves our faith. For example, when we are believing for something big, let's say a new church building, if we don't actively save toward our faith goal and maintain diligence in our budgeting so that our goal can become reality, we aren't really walking in faith. Someone might say, "Wait a minute, Pastor James, didn't you say that one couple miraculously stepped forward and paid the entire $3.5 million you needed to purchase your new building?" Yes, they did; however, that $3.5 million was the *balance* of what we needed to pay for the building in full. We'd already budgeted and saved a substantial amount toward that faith goal as a practical demonstration of our faith.

> *We believe God is an organized and orderly God, but when He wants to do a fresh work, we want to be ready for it with a margin of time.*

I would never discourage anyone who says they are believing God to "do it all," but I always balance my faith with the words of James 2:18: *But someone will say, "You have faith, and I have works." Show me your faith without your works, and I will show you my faith by my works.* To accomplish His purposes in the earth, God works in partnership with mankind, in accordance with the strategic principles laid out in His Word. If we steward according to His Word, creating the kind of margin that enables us to do what He's called us to do, when He says to do it, God always shows up in the midst of our faith projects. Though His Word never returns void, many are unwilling to do the work required to see a big faith project come to pass.

In chapter 1 I told how Tracy and I start each new year with goals; however, these goals are not put to paper until we feel God has spoken to us through His Word and in prayer. Only then do we get to work strategically planning for those things we believe for. If it's a bigger building, we have the God-given intelligence to understand that buildings cost money and sellers need down payments; therefore, we have a part to play in what God has called us to do. We stand on our faith, proving it by our works of creating margin, building it into our budgets, and making room for God to step in and perform His miracle.

We honor God when we choose to set aside provision for the vision He's given us. Big buildings come with big bills, so creating margin in preparation for the gift we anticipate receiving from the Lord gives us assurance the gift will not crush us financially when it arrives. If we are unprepared, we may wonder why we have to wait for our faith project to manifest when the truth is, God is waiting for us to get prepared to handle the blessing He has in store for us.

Though within the context of the business aspect of running a church, margin represents money, in God's economy margin is not limited to money. Margin can represent time, resources, thoughts, and smiles, to name a few. When we learn to create margin in every aspect of our lives, we will eliminate the number-one killer of people, relationships, businesses, and churches. That killer is *stress*.

For instance, when we pack our schedules to the point we have too much to do and not enough time to do it, we will never be available in those moments when God wants to use us to touch another's life. Perhaps we see someone in the supermarket and feel impressed to stop and pray for them, but we don't do it because of the time constraints we've put upon ourselves. We can create margin with our time.

Our diligence to create margin honors God and positions us for the miracles that are sure to come as we steward His gifts.

What about the times our children come home from school and just need to talk? Have we created margin for such instances, or do the ones we love most have to wait until Saturday because our weekday schedules are too packed? I speak from experience, having made this very mistake with each of my three daughters on more than one occasion. I've since learned the importance of creating margin with my time for family, work, church, and every aspect of my life.

Then there are the times when, at the end of the church service, the pastor seems to be spending a lot of time and energy talking about the importance of tithing and giving—a clear indication that he's stressed about paying this month's bills. No matter the source of stress, a life without margin is no way to live.

There is, without doubt, a higher level of strategic planning for us that gives God the opportunity to do extraordinary miracles. If we can show Him that we can be trusted with our resources, time, relationships, business, and churches, then He will blow our minds with all He can and will do for us.

The concept of margin is actually quite prophetic in that it's believing God can do something in the future bigger than what we can afford now. Margin entails preparation for the increase by sacrificing now for the goal to come. Margin involves hearing from God and then preparing for that God-given vision.

At Grow Church margin is non-negotiable, not only in our budget, but also in our service planning. For example, we believe God wants to show up at our weekend services; therefore, we prepare our order of service to fill an hour and fifteen minutes even though services are scheduled to last an hour and a half. That extra fifteen minutes allows the Holy Spirit to move without constraint. We believe God is an organized and orderly God, but when He wants to do a fresh work, we want to be ready for it with a margin of time.

Creating margin in our lives and finances always pays off. Doing so is hard work in the beginning, for needs are most always greater than income. However, our diligence to create margin honors God and positions us for the miracles that are sure to come as we steward His gifts.

Now for full disclosure: I've never experienced an instance when our margin *by itself* was enough to allow us to do what God called us to do, when He said to do it. But each time we've moved forward with another large faith project, God has always grown our margin and provided the additional resources we needed.

When we choose to establish a supernatural foundation of prayer, generosity, and margin in both our personal lives and churches or ministries, we will experience the peace of knowing we can always do what God calls us to do, when He says to do it.

CHAPTER TWO REVIEW:

1. Prayer, generosity, and margin are the key ingredients to success in ministry.

   » **CHALLENGE:** If you haven't done so in the past, I'm challenging you to consider the implementation of these three key ingredients.

2. Intercession, altar prayer, 21 days of prayer, and the prayer of salvation are all necessities for a church to be healthy and grow.

   » **CHALLENGE:** Start implementing training for all the different areas of prayer necessary to ensure the church is surrounded in prayer. Start talking about these initiatives more frequently, and the leaders will rise out of the congregation to participate.

3. A generosity strategy is imperative to healthy church growth.

   » **CHALLENGE:** Implement a generosity strategy that gives generously outside the church walls (local, national, and international). Partner with other organizations that already do it well so that you give, and they can do the work.

4. Margin may be the biggest missing key in most churches across the globe.

   » **CHALLENGE:** Start planning for a minimum 10 percent margin in your church budget.This will prepare you for what God has in mind to propel your church forward.

_____

_____

_____

_____

_____

_____

CHAPTER THREE

LEADERSHIP 101

"Those who fail to learn from history are
doomed to repeat it." —WINSTON CHURCHILL

"History cannot give us a program for the future, but it
can give us a fuller understanding of ourselves, and of our
common humanity, so that we can better face the future."
—ROBERT PENN WARREN

"A people without the knowledge of their past history,
origin, and culture is like a tree without roots."
—MARCUS GARVEY

I remember learning from some of my early ministry mentors that a pastor must be careful not to allow the sheep (church members) to get too close to him or her because, in these mentors' words, "sheep bite." Though I understood the concept, the idea of being the elite, untouchable pastor never sat well with me. So Tracy and I decided not to follow that recommended practice.

Ministry can be much more fun when the focus is on building meaningful relationships, which is exactly what we did. Yes, we've been hurt by some with whom we've had close relationships, but we never allowed those hurts to stop us from letting people into our hearts and continuing to build relationships. One good thing that came following those hurts and disappointments was a change in mindset as God showed us that we are to serve Him in our relationships. Once Tracy and I grasped this concept, we were set free.

Now if someone hurts us, instead of holding a grudge, we gather our thoughts and pray, not only for the one who hurt us, but also for our hearts to be healed. We found that when we prayed for someone, we couldn't simultaneously hold a grudge against them. Praying for those who have caused us pain is scriptural, for Jesus said, *"And whenever you stand praying, if you have anything against anyone, forgive him, that your Father in heaven may also forgive you your trespasses"* (Mark 11:24).

The only way to build an effective ministry is to build an effective team of people. And the only way to build an effective team of people is by building real relationships in which people can become close. Relationships can't be real unless they embrace vulnerability, which means they are capable of inflicting hurt. The only way to lead a ministry team is to allow people to be close. Without this closeness, each person will rely on his or her own ideas about the ministry and the direction it should go. For this reason, at Grow Church we cherish close relationships that allow us to build big, strong teams—both of staff members and volunteers.

Though God didn't create humankind to be individual islands unto ourselves, it's easy to tend toward this kind of life and leadership. From an early age we hear people say things like this: "Nobody is going to focus on your success better than you," "If you want to get something done, do it yourself," and "Nobody cares as much about a business as its owner." Though these may be factual statements within the context of building a business, they are certainly not true when it comes to establishing a church and building other leaders.

Falling into the all-too-common pattern of filling needs is a real challenge for churches, especially when there is much to be accomplished.

As pastors, we can't win in ministry without moving toward positive relationships with our leadership teams. Sadly, I've seen some pastors and church leaders whose motive for building relationships is to bring on board others who will help get them where they want to go. At Grow Church we don't use people as means to achieve *our* goals. Instead, we discover the gifts, talents, and purposes God has instilled into each individual and then help them achieve *their* goals. In so doing, the byproduct of their success is that the church achieves its goals.

The local church is the best place to set people up to succeed in God's purpose for them. God created the local church so that people would have a place to develop their God-given gifts and talents; however, most churches don't operate this way. For instance, when I was a young volunteer looking for a place to serve at my church, I remember someone telling me I was meant to be an usher. I wasn't particularly a "people person," nor was I knowledgeable about logistics; rather, the church had need of ushers—and I was fresh meat. Nobody took time to get to know me, to understand my purpose or calling; they just wanted to plug me in where they had a need.

Falling into the all-too-common pattern of filling needs is a real challenge for churches, especially when there is much to be accomplished. But at Grow Church we purpose to identify the gifts and talents God has placed within each person and then point them toward *their* purpose within the church.

THE "YOU FIRST" PRINCIPLE OF RELATIONAL LEADERSHIP

> *Let nothing be done through selfish ambition or conceit,*
> *but in lowliness of mind let each esteem others better than*
> *himself. Let each of you look out not only for his own interests,*
> *but also for the interests of others* (PHILIPPIANS 2:3–4).

In the early days of establishing Grow Church, my wife and I knew the importance of building both leadership teams and volunteer teams through establishing healthy personal relationships. That's why we invited every new person to our home for dinner.

We were acutely aware that others in our situation might view the opportunity as a means to answer the question, "What's in it for me?" For this reason, Tracy and I were deliberate in keeping the focus on our guests, their goals, and how we could help them get there. We knew if we were not intentional in developing relationships with our potential future church leadership, they would not be able to do the same for others as the church grew.

As lead pastors, Tracy and I had to set the example of what we named the "You First" principle of leadership, which we define as "You do it first (model it), and then your teams will also do it." We've learned that it always takes time to model the values and actions we want others to emulate, but the results are always well worth the effort.

I once heard a well-known pastor say that new pastors should not hold back their cell numbers from people in their ministry until membership reaches two thousand people. I remember thinking to myself, *That sounds crazy!* But I now agree with his statement. If a pastor is too hard to reach too early in the life of the church, he or she will never be able to train the leadership team in healthy relationships so that they can take over as the church grows. To create a leadership team (or any team) that knows how to build relationships, it's vital to model the You First principle. Then, when it's time to minimize the number of people who have access to your cell number, your leadership team can take over the necessary roles in supporting those who may need your help. If done correctly, this transition should happen organically.

Many pastors who want the transition to take place early actually miss out on a vital element of pastoring: the miracles God performs in leaders during the time of their development, which I refer to as "the grind." It was during our own grind that God formed in my wife and me a great heart for people, which we then instilled into our leadership team. I vividly remember the time we learned a church member had been hospitalized, and for the first time since we became lead pastors, Tracy and I did not receive the initial call to someone at Grow Church. We were also not the second call they made; instead, they called the leader of the small group they attended. That's when we knew we were on the road to success when it came to people building relationships and serving each other with their God-given gifts.

Growing a healthy church is wildly satisfying, though a growing church presents its own logistical challenges. For instance, when Grow Church added a second Sunday service, Tracy and I continued to go to the lobby following each service to greet the people. According to our leadership staff, our doing so created bottlenecks in both the lobby and the parking lot between services. The staff was also concerned we might be too accessible to people who might take advantage of our limited time; therefore, they recommended we discontinue the practice.

We understood their concerns and appreciated their protective stance in our behalf, but to this day we still go to the lobby so that those who want to meet us or tell us something going on in their lives are free to do so. This simple but consistent modeling of the You First principle of relational leadership has helped us in our volunteer team-building efforts. People have told our staff literally hundreds of times, "The lead pastors are always so accessible." What an honor it is to hear those words. I don't ever want to lose the personal connection to the people God has called us to pastor.

Though our desire is to be accessible to people, the reality is, due to the size of Grow Church, it is no longer possible for Tracy and me to handle all pastoral care issues that arise. We've created an exceptional pastoral and leadership team to attend to these matters, and many of our team members possess gifts that make them better suited than we are to helping people. Tracy and I purpose to be open about our need to refer people to our pastoral and leadership team, which helps build trust in people that they are in the best hands for their needs.

To understand relational leadership, I recommend reading *The Way of the Shepherd* by Dr. Kevin Leman and Bill Pentak. We took our staff through this book weekly for a season to help them better understand leadership from a relational level. As we explored the concepts in the book, we consistently modeled the You First principle.

LEADER: LEAD BY EXAMPLE!

Follow my example, as I follow the example of Christ.
I praise you for remembering me in everything
and for holding to the traditions just as I passed
them on to you (1 CORINTHIANS 11:1–2).

Effective leaders have a way of inspiring people with their words—words that oftentimes outlive those who initially spoke them and then go on to inspire future generations. For instance, when Franklin D. Roosevelt took the helm of our nation in 1933, the country was in a deep depression. At his inauguration he assured Americans, saying, "The only thing we have to fear is fear itself."

In 1961 John F. Kennedy inspired the nation with these words: "Ask not what your country can do for you, ask what you can do for your country." And perhaps the most compelling words of the last century came from Dr. Martin Luther King's 1963 speech, "I Have a Dream," in which he boldly declared, "Free at last. Free at last. Thank God Almighty, we are free at last!"

> *I've seen numerous churches try to establish small groups without the lead pastor's direct involvement, and none were a success.*

As inspiring as these words were—and still are—the fact of the matter is that no leader can lead a group of people by words alone. Concepts, principles, and culture must be *modeled* because, when it comes to leadership, people don't care as much about what you say as about what they see you do. Leaders who are unwilling to model what they want their followers to do are fighting an uphill battle and are unlikely to make it to the finish line of their callings.

Throughout my own life and ministry, I've seen a lot of "leading from the top." What I mean by this term is that leaders would tell people what to do but wouldn't do it themselves. I've served under leaders who were harsh, yet told us not to be harsh. They protected their time instead of building relationships, yet told us not to protect our time. I don't mean to be critical, because these leaders were only doing what they were trained to do. I had to retrain myself to think and act as God thinks and acts, just as Jesus did. He said, *"Most assuredly, I say to you, the Son can do nothing of Himself, but what He sees the Father do; for whatever He does, the Son also does in like manner"* (John 5:19). Jesus modeled for His followers the behavior His Father had modeled for Him.

I've learned that when it comes to introducing a new concept to those I lead, I must first have changed my own disciplines with the intention of implementing new behaviors for the *rest of my life*. Only then can I successfully model the new behavior—usually for a year—before actively making it part of our church culture. Operating this way is a huge commitment, but the investment of time and energy is well worth it. As leaders, we should never tell people to do something we aren't already doing; we should lead by what we do more than by what we say, always mindful of the You First principle.

When Grow Church had grown to a size that prohibited Tracy and me from inviting new members to our home, we asked our leadership team and staff members to invite those new people to their homes for dinner. However, we didn't really have to do much asking, because they had watched us model that behavior for several years.

Though Grow Church has experienced exponential growth in recent years, our foundational concept is that a church must grow both smaller and larger at the same time. I know this state-ment sounds like an oxymoron, but it isn't. It's simply our way of saying that personal connections will always be a vital part of our culture, no matter the size of the church.

People want to be loved and know they are cared for, which is why we so highly esteem building relationships within the church. Two of the ways we do this, both of which are examples of the church growing smaller, is through our Grow Groups and Grow Teams. Both are great places for emerging leadership to model what they've learned from their own leaders as they encourage the building of relationships.

Grow Groups are our church's version of a small group, which is modeled for us throughout the entire New Testament. Speaking of the early apostles, the Bible says, *Day after day ... from house to house, they never stopped teaching and proclaiming the good news that Jesus is the Messiah* (Acts 5:42). Most of the early local churches started with this concept of small groups meeting in homes. I believe churches today miss a blessing when they do not actively engage in small meetings held outside the church, sometime between Monday and Saturday, for that is where long-lasting relationships are built and meaningful life change occurs.

I personally believe small groups are a success *only* when the lead pastor or pastors are involved. For instance, when we launched our first small groups at Grow Church, Tracy and I led three of them until other leaders were ready to take what we'd modeled for them into their own groups. I've seen numerous churches try to establish small groups without the lead pastor's direct involvement, and none were a success. Small groups need a full buy-in from top leadership to be successful.

Our Grow Teams also serve as places to build relationships. Grow Teams are small groups of people in intentional relationships built around their similar giftings. Teams serve in various areas during our weekend services, such as in the parking lot, as greeters and ushers, in production and photography, at the bookstore, and everyplace else where their gifts are needed to ensure an excellent experience for those in attendance. Again, we don't build our teams based on the church's needs; we find each person's gifts and talents and then connect them with other like-minded people in an area where they can establish long-term relationships and experience fulfillment.

I tell our leaders if they will first build relationships and then train their teams to build them as well, they will not be disappointed.

Whether an individual is leading a Grow Group or a Grow Team, it is important that these leaders have a means to measure their success. We teach our leaders the way to do this is to (1) keep track of the times they are the first person to know about an issue or emergency in one of their group members' or team members' lives, and (2) over the course of their team building, see if this practice tapers off. If the calls taper off, they are doing a good job in training their team to support each other.

I've found that most people's maximum capacity of individuals who consider them a leader and can call them when a need arises is fifty. At that point, it's time for the leader to multiply his or her impact by releasing new leaders to model for others what they've modeled for their teams.

Dale Carnegie's book *How to Win Friends and Influence People* was first published in 1936, yet it remains one of the top-selling self-help books ever written. In it he lists these eight vital criteria for building healthy relationships:

1. Do not criticize.
2. Give honest, sincere appreciation.
3. Get the other person's point of view and see things from his or her angle.
4. Become genuinely interested in other people.
5. Smile.
6. Remember names.
7. Be a good listener.
8. Make the other person feel important.

I tell our leaders if they will first build relationships and then train their teams to build them as well, they will not be disappointed. That's why, at Grow Church, we highly value the You First principle of relational leadership, and we model it at every level of leadership within our growing organization.

1. Building meaningful relationships with members of your congregation is important to sustained growth in ministry.

   » **CHALLENGE:** Create a plan of action to tell stories to your staff about relationships you are building with people in your congregation. Challenge staff members to do the same and then, to keep the action plan in front of them at all times, ask them each week how they are doing in this area.

2. Your discipleship track within your church might need a fresh assessment to see if it is connecting people to their purpose within your volunteer teams.

   » **CHALLENGE:** Assess and be ready to modify your current discipleship track to discover the gifts within people and help them use their gifts to build the kingdom within your church.

3. You may feel like there is a heavy weight of responsibility on you as a pastor, and you are right. However, there are ways to start empowering others to help carry the responsibility.

   » **CHALLENGE:** Evaluate the amount of time it currently takes you, personally, to elevate people within your ministry. Distribute some of that weight to your staff and follow up with them frequently.

4. A fresh challenge to your staff might be necessary to propel them forward in raising up other leaders within their volunteer teams.

   » **CHALLENGE:** Recommend a book that might encourage your staff's success in this area. Two examples are *The Way of the Shepherd* and *How to Win Friends and Influence People*.

   _____

   _____

   _____

   _____

A HEALTHY CULTURE BUILDS HEALTHY TEAMS

"There's no magic formula for great company culture. The key is just to treat your staff how you would like to be treated." —RICHARD BRANSON

"If your culture doesn't like geeks, you're in real trouble." —BILL GATES

"The culture of a company is the sum of the behaviors of its people." —MICHAEL KOULY

"Great things ... are never done by one person. They're done by a team of people." —STEVE JOBS

Healthy teams, both staff and volunteers, are built upon the foundation of a healthy church culture. A church's culture, good or bad, happens either by default or by design. That's why, at Grow Church, rather than allowing our feelings, our upbringing, or the standards of society to determine our culture, we intentionally and consistently create the culture we want to see.

The Lord spoke through the prophet Isaiah and said, *"Forget the former things; do not dwell on the past. See, I am doing a new thing! Now it springs up; do you not perceive it?"* (Isaiah 43:18–19). Whether your church background is Pentecostal, Charismatic, Catholic, Baptist, Wesleyan, or any other denomination, you'll probably agree that your church culture has been much the same since you were young. We understand businesses need to change to stay on top of the market, but this idea of healthy change has escaped most of the church world.

Though the Lord *is the same yesterday, today, and forever* (Hebrews 13:8), He is always doing new things. For instance, the American big tent revivals of the late 1800s and the 1900s are behind us, yet revival remains present in many churches; it just doesn't look the same as it once did. Unfortunately, some people take a judgmental view of growing churches because their processes and approach to ministry are the polar opposite of the traditional way things were once done.

It's always wise to approach tradition with a wary eye, for Jesus said, *Thus you nullify the word of God by your tradition that you have handed down* (Mark 7:13 NIV). Though the message of the gospel hasn't changed, the method in which it is proclaimed certainly has. I appreciate new ideas and ways to reach people. I appreciate changes in the approach to reach an ever-changing culture. If the Church, meaning the global body of Christ, is unwilling to change its methods of reaching people, local churches will become without cultural relevance and empty.

We have this saying at Grow Church: "We will never change our message, but we will always change our methods in leading people to Jesus, reaching our community, and giving and sharing." Many of our systems, processes, and methods undergo change when we find they don't match our culture. Though a culture guide was not necessary in the beginning, as the church grew and our culture became more defined, we wanted a way to preserve and protect the culture God had developed.

When you take the time to establish your church or ministry's culture, language, and phrases unique to your organization ... you're truly establishing a healthy trajectory for future growth.

Our Grow Church culture guide is a valuable tool that allows us to communicate our culture to our growing leadership team, staff, and volunteer teams. It ensures that our unique and healthy culture is infused into all those who serve with their gifts and talents. Though a culture guide should never be taken from another organization because it needs to reflect an organization's unique heart and values, I'm going to share portions of our culture guide to assist you in writing your own.

GROW CHURCH CULTURE

1. **WE ARE TRANSFORMED BY GOD'S PRESENCE.**
   - IT'S ABOUT: *Knowing Him.*

2. **WE VALUE PEOPLE & DEMONSTRATE IT WITH OUR ACTIONS.**
   - IT'S ABOUT: *Loving Well.*

3. **WE KNOW EXCELLENCE ISN'T BY ACCIDENT.**
   - IT'S ABOUT: *Being Intentional.*

4. **WE INSPIRE OTHERS WITH AUTHENTICITY, NOT PERFECTION.**
   - IT'S ABOUT: *Embracing Transparency.*

5. **WE IDENTIFY POTENTIAL & CULTIVATE IT.**
   - IT'S ABOUT: *Empowering Others.*

6. **WE ACTIVELY PURSUE WAYS TO GROW.**
   - IT'S ABOUT: *Teachable Attitudes.*

7. **WE SEEK OPPORTUNITIES TO BE A BLESSING.**
   - IT'S ABOUT: *Generous Living.*

8. **WE PARTY WITH A PURPOSE.**
   - IT'S ABOUT: *Having Fun.*

GROW CHURCH LANGUAGE CULTURE

DON'T SAY ...	INSTEAD SAY ...
Your church	Our church
My team	Our team
My group	Our group
Volunteer	Team member
Small group	Grow Group
Band/singers	Worship team
I have to do it.	I get to do it.
I have to be there.	I get to be there.
The time you have to arrive	Your call time
Sorry, I know serving is hard.	Thank you for serving!

GROW CHURCH CULTURAL PHRASES

EVERY MIRACLE STARTS WITH A PROBLEM. You can't have one without the other. We don't stay upset when there are problems; instead, we move into excitement for what God is going to do in the midst of our situation.

WE MAKE IT TOGETHER, AND WE MISS IT TOGETHER. We are a team. If we share the wins, we also share our misses. If we see that something is not going the right direction, we jump in and help.

EAT PASTA WHILE IT'S HOT. We don't procrastinate with people. If we see an open door to connect or impact a life, we take it. We don't let someone's excitement cool off by waiting around; we get the person connected immediately. This proactive approach extends beyond our interactions with people, because we realize procrastination will cool any project or momentum.

WE DON'T "HAVE TO"; WE "GET TO." We realize that it's a privilege to be used by God in any capacity. We serve willingly. We show up with a smile and expect that as we build God's house, miracles will take place.

WE ARE NOT A CHURCH WITH SMALL GROUPS; WE ARE A CHURCH OF SMALL GROUPS. Grow Groups are not just additional programming we offer at church. They are the heartbeat of the community we are cultivating. Our goal is that 100 percent of Grow Church would be involved in groups.

REAL-LIFE CHANGE HAPPENS IN THE CONTEXT OF RELATIONSHIPS. When we do life with people, we grow. When we're in a Grow Group, it establishes a consistent peer group of support and creates real relationships that challenge us.

CHILDREN'S MINISTRY IS NOT BABYSITTING; IT'S LEADERSHIP DEVELOPMENT. We might play games, but we're not playing games when it comes to our kids. We're intentionally building the next generation of leaders.

DON'T PARENT ALONE. Some say it takes a village to raise a child. Our kids learn from everything they see, so we might as well have them in environments that will support the godly values we want in our children.

NOTHING CHANGES WITHOUT PRAYER. Prayer is how we invite God into our situations. It's the Spirit of God who does the work to bring the change we desire.

SUPER ON THE NATURAL. God puts His "super" on our "natural" to make what we do supernatural.

INSPECT WHAT YOU EXPECT. We make clear expectations and follow up with inspections. We mean what we say and follow it up with action. Where there's accountability, there's trust and growth.

BELIEVE THE BEST. We protect ourselves against division, fighting, and ultimately wasting time by believing the best about others in all situations that can appear otherwise.

WHO DID YOU MEET? It's easy to get lost in the tasks during a service. So we literally ask each other, "Who did you meet?" This keeps us accountable to be people focused on the weekends.

SEE IT; SAY IT. We don't keep our encouragement to ourselves. We are not stingy with our praises. If we see something good or praiseworthy, we say it.

EMPTY HELL AND FILL HEAVEN. We are reminded that we, as believers, have a real and urgent calling to fill heaven with souls who have accepted Jesus as their Savior.

GOD DOESN'T MAKE JUNK. We are God's masterpieces. He doesn't make junk; therefore, we should view ourselves as loved and full of potential.

When you take the time to establish your church or ministry's culture, language, and phrases unique to your organization—and then put them in writing—you're truly establishing a healthy trajectory for future growth.

CHAPTER FOUR REVIEW:

1. Healthy, growing churches find ways to never change the message, but always change their methods of communication, which could be anything from welcome videos, to discipleship track simplification, to communicating announcements from the stage, to name a few.

   » **CHALLENGE:** Consider comparing your methods to other, larger churches to see if there is a communication tactic you are currently using that could use an adjustment to meet the needs of a broader audience.

2. Healthy church culture is crucial to your organization's success and future growth.

   » **CHALLENGE:** Write out your church culture the way that you currently see it, and then select three-to-five other staff members to help you critique it. Reduce the material to something easily communicated to others, and then start talking about it weekly within your staff meetings.

3. Establishing a list of cultural phrases is a fun way to allow people to see behind the curtain of ministry a little bit and start to understand how you speak. This will help your staff turn into an inclusive team rather than an exclusive team.

   » **CHALLENGE:** Ask your staff what phrases are normal for you, but not normal for a person who might be visiting for the first time. This will be a fun project that will help visitors feel welcome and then eventually become part of a volunteer team more quickly.

_____

_____

_____

_____

_____

ACCOUNTABILITY: ESSENTIAL FOR A HEALTHY CHURCH

"An accountability partner is able to perceive what you can't see when blind spots and weaknesses block your vision. Such a person serves as a tool in God's hand to promote spiritual growth, and he or she watches out for your best interest." —CHARLES STANLEY

"You are accountable for your actions, your decisions, your life; no one else is, but you." —CATHERINE PULSIFER

"Accountability breeds response-ability."
—STEPHEN R. COVEY

"A body of men holding themselves accountable to nobody ought not to be trusted by anybody." —THOMAS PAINE

Accountability is a highly valued characteristic within our organization. Whatever our level of leadership within the church, we're only as good as the accountability that surrounds and protects us. Without accountability, we set ourselves up for failure.

As lead pastors, my wife and I expect all members of our staff to hold themselves accountable to others. I'm not talking about their being accountable to us; rather, they each need a group of trusted people who will ask the hard questions about their lives and ministries.

I'm going to describe how accountability looks within Grow Church, but these guidelines will work for anyone and everyone.

I recommend every person have three layers of people, with each layer consisting of three people, around them for optimal mental, emotional, and spiritual health. The first layer of three people is made up of those considered ahead of the individual in that they have more experience in business, ministry, and life in general. The second level consists of three people considered to be the individual's peers, who are near the same age and have similar life experience and purpose. The third layer of three are those behind who haven't yet progressed to the life level of the individual, though they are striving to get there. Each of these three levels is important because each of us have the need to be poured into by mentors and also to pour into others as their mentor.

The people we consider to be ahead of us need to know we've invited them to be in that position so that they are comfortable in asking us the hard questions and telling us things that may be difficult but necessary to our health. If you do not have this kind of accountability in place, you need to establish it right away. Ask God whom you should reach out to, and then do it.

I recommend communicating once a month with each of these individuals for their insight and wisdom.

Remember, the people you choose to mentor you should already have relationship with you. If you don't yet have these relationships in your life, then pursue them. Once you've established the relationships, you can then invite them to pour into you.

BYLAWS FOR A HEALTHY CHURCH

Be shepherds of God's flock that is under your care,
watching over them—not because you must, but because
you are willing, as God wants you to be; not pursuing
dishonest gain, but eager to serve (1 PETER 5:2 NIV).

Though my wife, Tracy, and I are the lead pastors of Grow Church, we do not believe we should have all the decision-making authority in the church. Should one or both of us leave or be replaced, there needs to be a healthy foundation in place to ensure Grow Church's survival.

The church is not ours; it's God's—and He will protect it. He will allow us to lead it while we are healthy enough to do so; however, in looking to the future, we put in place bylaws that would outlast both of us and our staff. A *bylaw* is a rule adopted by an organization for the government of its members and regulation of its affairs. Our Grow Church bylaws outline healthy church roles and responsibilities from a fiduciary standpoint.

Though I've always engaged an attorney to set up bylaws for our previous ministries, one of the resource organizations we found most helpful in setting up our Grow Church bylaws was StartChurch (StartChurch.com), which offers step-by-step resources and software integral to correctly setting up a church and protecting it. They've helped us stay on top of changes in the law that applied to us, offered suggestions regarding our bylaws, and in general have kept us safe.

EXECUTIVE LEADERSHIP

Where no wise guidance is, the people fall, but in the multitude of counselors there is safety (PROVERBS 11:14 AMPC).

The day-to-day responsibility of decisions within Grow Church belongs to the senior pastor and the executive pastor, who are the president and vice president (respectively) of our organization. Tracy is the senior pastor and president, and I'm executive pastor and vice president; however, we work together as the lead pastors of Grow Church, sharing responsibilities for the day-to-day operations of the church. These responsibilities include overseeing weekly meetings, giving reviews, and growing each area of ministry.

In Grow Church culture, leadership is not set up as a "from the top down" structure; rather, my wife and I lead the church *with* our staff leadership team. However, there is an order of accountability we follow in the best interest of the church, which I will now share.

OVERSEERS

Since an overseer manages God's household, he must be blameless—not overbearing, not quick tempered, not given to drunkenness, not violent, not pursuing dishonest gain (TITUS 1:7 NIV).

Grow Church bylaws define our *overseers* as "advisory counsel to the lead pastors" and specifically to the senior pastor.

As lead pastors, Tracy and I are accountable to our overseers, who are our spiritual mentors as well as our spiritual fathers. Our overseers ensure our health as leaders and provide guidance when we need it. The interesting thing about them is that they are pastors of other congregations. They are the ones who ask, "James and Tracy, how are you doing?" and then follow up that question with, "No, how are you *really* doing?" They know us well and always have our backs; however, they will always ask the hard questions and challenge our leadership when they visit Grow Church, usually on an annual basis.

We've learned, for a church to have healthy pastors, the pastors must have trusted overseers.

Our overseers are prepared to serve in an additional role if necessary. Should either of us have a moral failure or should a need arise to transition the role of senior pastor, the overseers would step in to help with that transition.

Though we are accountable to our overseers, they have no authority in directing the church or in its day-to-day operations. Even so, our trustees hold the overseers in high regard and may, from time to time, ask them for advice concerning fiduciary decisions. So while the trustees serve as our fiduciary entity, the overseers serve as our spiritual accountability entity, which creates a good balance for Tracy and me as lead pastors.

We've learned, for a church to have healthy pastors, the pastors must have trusted overseers.

TRUSTEES

This is a trustworthy saying: "If someone aspires to be a church leader, he desires an honorable position." So a church leader must be a man whose life is above reproach. He must be faithful to his wife. He must exercise self-control, live wisely, and have a good reputation (1 TIMOTHY 3:1–2 NLT).

Our trustees are business- and church-savvy individuals who have been with us a long time. Giving of both their time and their finances, the trustees are completely invested in the church's success. They serve on volunteer teams during the weekend services and are always highly involved so that they stay aware of the state of the flock as the church continues to grow.

Our trustees carry the responsibility of fiduciary guidance for Grow Church. As such, they approve all budgets, leases, and capital expenditures, along with any large purchases for the church. They approve these expenses either by way of budget and capital expenditure approval or on an as-needed basis such as an important project outside normal spending that comes up between scheduled trustee meetings. The trustees have long-standing relationships with other business professionals.

Many churches make the mistake of placing people with ministry experience on their boards of trustees.

Though the trustees do not make day-to-day decisions, they approve the larger budget the executive pastor presents to them prior to the close of the fiscal year. Trustees can challenge that budget, approve it, question it, or turn it down.

Tracy and I meet monthly with our board of trustees to review these and other additional items:

- Income statement (P&L)
- Balance sheet
- Year-to-date budget vs. actual budget
- Attendance and income graphs
- Year-over-year numbers
- Pertinent financial issues or initiatives
- New updates on special projects
- Ministry updates
- Upcoming events and initiatives
- Marketing initiatives
- Safety issues and updates
- Any up-to-date walk-on items that require input

When it comes to selecting a board of trustees for the church, the number-one attribute to look for in a potential trustee is that he or she is already invested in the church. Without this investment a trustee would not have the ability to make appropriate decisions when faced with challenging circumstances.

Our trustees have business, pastoral, and legal backgrounds, along with other experience beneficial to the financial health of our church.

Once we began the process of selecting our board of trustees, we had some specific characteristics we looked for in each person:

- A trustee should love God, love us, and love the vision of Grow Church.

- A trustee should be a man or woman we had relationship with who had earned our trust and who possessed a lot of business experience.

- A trustee should be a giver, invested in the work we were creating so that he or she could make the best decisions in behalf of the church as we moved forward.

- A trustee should agree with church doctrine, tithing, and giving offerings, as well as the Give-Save-Live principle (see chapter 7, Biblical Stewardship).

- A trustee should operate his or her business in a godly fashion.

- A trustee should honor his or her spouse.

- A trustee should serve on a volunteer team at church so that people see he or she is interested in being part of a team rather than being "boss."

Our trustees have business, pastoral, and legal backgrounds, along with other experience beneficial to the financial health of our church. Importantly, our board of trustees is a *voting board* as opposed to an *advisory board*. This simply means they do not advise executive leadership on their decisions; rather, they vote only on fiduciary matters concerning Grow Church.

Many churches make the mistake of placing people with ministry experience on their boards of trustees. While ministry experience is also crucial to a church's success, these gifted individuals are better suited to pastoral care and the oversight of the state of the flock or a spiritual advisory role than as a trustee.

I've been on boards where the members were difficult to serve with and not much fun. Our board of trustees is quite different from such boards, in that they love Jesus with all they have and support Grow Church with everything they have. Our trustees are amazing leaders who help us steer this ship past the rocks.

PASTORS AND DIRECTORS

Preach the word; be prepared in season and out of season; correct, rebuke and encourage—with great patience and careful instruction (2 TIMOTHY 4:2 NIV).

After the trustees, come the pastors and directors. This group is responsible for the day-to-day operations of Grow Church. Pastors and directors meet weekly to push the ministry forward and help it get better and better.

Most of our pastors are volunteers unless they serve in a director role that requires them to build teams and be accountable to office hours and a job description. My wife and I lead this team, and all pastors and directors report to us.

The difference between a pastor and a director is this: A pastor uses his or her God-given gift to pastor people according to the Word of God. A director leads volunteers and staff to accomplish the purpose, task, and execution of the ministry objectives in his or her department.

DIRECTORS

In everything set them an example by doing what is good. In your teaching show integrity, seriousness and soundness of speech that cannot be condemned, so that those who oppose you may be ashamed because they have nothing bad to say about us (TITUS 2:7–8).

Our directors all have annual goals and are accountable for growing their areas of ministry. Some of their areas of ministry include children, students, young adults, teams, groups, facilities, and discipleship, to name a few. Not only do we challenge our directors, we also help them grow their areas of ministry throughout the year. As a result of our commitment to their success, we've experienced only minimal turnover in this level of leadership. This small turnover is a good thing, because great turnover brings questions from members of the church family who may not understand how difficult it is to successfully run ministry operations.

We've set up a continuing education allotment of funds for our full-time directors to help further their education or training so that they are always growing and getting better. As lead pastors, my wife and I believe that when we are serious about something, the best way to show our support is to back it financially. Continuing education is just one way we show our support.

We like to get our directors out of the office throughout the year so that they can stay fresh and build great volunteer teams in their departments. We take all our directors to an annual, out-of-town team-building conference so that we can build our relationships while we experience leadership training together. Doing so is imperative to growth as a leadership team. As the saying goes, Those who play together stay together.

Finally, our directors get fifteen days paid time off annually and an additional week off for an approved mission trip. My wife and I endeavor to be actively involved in each of their lives, though doing so becomes more challenging as the church grows.

ACCOUNTABLE TO THE VISION: THE BIG 4

When there is no clear prophetic vision, people quickly wander astray. But when you follow the revelation of the Word, heaven's bliss fills your soul (PROVERBS 29:18 TPT).

At Grow Church we have great people serving as overseers, trustees, and staff members, each of whom value the relationships of accountability the church is established upon. But even more importantly, we value and are accountable to the God-given vision that serves as our church's foundation. Simply put, our vision is *to transform lives with the message of Jesus Christ.*

Having a God-given vision is vital; however, that vision cannot come to pass without a corresponding mission. Our mission, which we define as how we do the vision, is to create environments that engage people in their next steps to fulfill their purpose. Then we define how we do the mission as this: (1) *know God*, (2) *find freedom*, (3) *discover their purpose, and* (4) *make a difference.* We refer to these four components of our mission as the "Big 4," the filter through which Tracy and I, as well as our leadership team and staff, view every decision we make. Any Grow Church initiative—whether it be an area of ministry within the church or a mission endeavor outside the church—must fit within the scope of the Big 4 or we don't do it.

Every church needs to have a clearly stated vision and mission—but it also must have a strategic process, or strategic steps, to fulfill its mission. Here's what the process looks like at Grow Church:

MISSION	PROCESS
Help people know God	Weekend services (*worship, prayer, teaching*)
Help people find freedom	Grow Groups (*specific topics in a home-group setting*)
Help people discover purpose	Grow Steps (*beginning of the discipleship process*)
Help people make a difference	Grow Teams (*serving on a weekend volunteer team*)

Local churches are vital to the health of communities, yet many churches try to be *everything* to their communities. We know Grow Church can best serve our community by doing the things we are good at and that are in line with our vision, and then by financially supporting the endeavors others are called to do. This setup allows for excellence in our initiatives so that we don't get outside of what God has called us to do.

For example, when Tracy and I first established Grow Church, we had a food pantry at the church so that we could help people in need. The food pantry was great idea for sure, especially since Jesus spoke of feeding the hungry, saying, "*Assuredly, I say to you, inasmuch as you did it to one of the least of these My brethren, you did it to Me*" (Matthew 25:40); however, it didn't take us long to discover we were not good at operating a food pantry. Not only was our good idea draining resources, but our good intentions also made little impact on the community.

When we ran the idea of our food pantry through the lens of the Big 4, we realized God had not called us to do a food pantry, so we quickly corrected course. We established a relationship with an existing local food pantry that we sponsor not only financially but also with our monthly "serve events" in which our members have the opportunity to volunteer.

Healthy churches are built upon healthy foundations of accountability—and Grow Church is no exception. We have built accountability into every aspect of ministry but perhaps nowhere more so than in our finances, as we are about to see.

CHAPTER FIVE REVIEW:

1. **We are only as good as our accountability.**

   » **CHALLENGE:** Find three people you trust to speak truth to you, who are more accomplished than you in ministry. Also, find three people around the same position as you in ministry whom you can glean from. Let each of them know they are selected for this position in your life.

2. **Bylaws keep organizations safe.**

   » **CHALLENGE:** Create (if you don't have them) or review your current bylaws to make sure they are updated and written in such a way to keep you and the organization safe.

3. **Selecting well-seasoned businessmen and businesswomen with a heart for Jesus and the church is the best way to structure your board of trustees.**

   » **CHALLENGE:** Evaluate the level of business expertise obtained by members of your board of trustees. If you find a lack of experience, you can rearrange current members to different areas of the ministry or invite new people with business expertise onto your board to add what is missing to the group.

4. **People most always choose to get behind and support a well-cast vision as opposed to supporting a need.**

   » **CHALLENGE:** If you find that you frequently need to ask for money from your congregation or to raise funds, you may have a vision problem rather than a money problem. Consider "re-visioning" your church and better communicating that vision to your congregation.

_____

_____

_____

BUILDING A HEALTHY OUTLOOK ON FINANCES

"We must consult our means rather than our wishes."
—GEORGE WASHINGTON

A budget is telling your money where to go instead of wondering where it went." —DAVE RAMSEY

"You don't have to see the whole staircase, just take the first step." —MARTIN LUTHER KING, JR.

"The desire of power in excess caused the angels to fall; the desire of knowledge in excess caused man to fall; but in charity there is no excess; neither can angel nor man come in danger by it." —SIR FRANCIS BACON

As I sat at my desk listening to the young missionary seated opposite me, whom I'll refer to as Carrie, the somber look on her face bore little resemblance to the excited young woman Grow Church had launched into the mission field only two years earlier.

Carrie was one of our own, having come out of serving in our children's ministry with an assignment to serve as a missionary for a foundation established by another church, whose pastors and leadership team were great friends of ours. Not only was Grow Church a significant contributor to the foundation, but we were also Carrie's sending church.

Now, back in Naples to raise funds so that she could continue her work, she said, "Pastor James, I received some very tough news that could possibly prevent me from going back onto the mission field." I had no idea where she was going with that statement, so I listened patiently as she explained that the mission organization had changed some of its guidelines for missionaries.

When Carrie had initially entered the mission field, the organization didn't require their missionaries to have a savings account, emergency fund, or a retirement plan in place. The new changes, however, required missionaries to have all three in place before they entered the field. Additionally, due to inflation there was also a rise in expenses such as travel tickets, taxi transportation, and unexpected trips home from the mission field. Each of these items are necessary parts of a mission-field budget, which Carrie hadn't initially considered. As a result of the changes, her costs had gone up, and she needed to raise an additional six to eight hundred dollars per month to return to the mission field.

As is typical of most missionaries, Carrie wanted to give everything she had to the work God had called her to do. Most missionaries, including Carrie, are selfless people typically uncomfortable with the idea of raising money for themselves, though it is necessary for their wellbeing. She wasn't interested in making money, and as far as savings, an emergency fund, or retirement were concerned, well, God would provide.

God never works on only one thing at a time ... He is always working for our good

I agree with the biblical principle of God's provision, for the Word of God clearly says, *And my God shall supply all your need according to His riches in glory by Christ Jesus* (Philippians 4:19), but I also believe God gave each of us a brain and an enormous amount of wisdom we are to use to lead our lives. When I told Carrie I agreed with the organization's approach and that the new rules were God's wisdom for her and the others, I could see the disappointment on her face when she said, "So then, I can't go back?"

I used her question as a teaching opportunity. I told her the new rules were not intended to keep her from returning to the mission field; rather, they were to ensure her needs were supplied in a way that would enable her to continue her work for as long as she was called to do so. And for good measure, I read 2 Corinthians 9:8 from the Amplified Bible, Classic Edition: *And God is able to make all grace (every favor and earthly blessing) come to you in abundance, so that you may always and under all circumstances and whatever the need be self-sufficient [possessing enough to require no aid or support and furnished in abundance for every good work and charitable donation].* Without this level of self-sufficiency, the body of Christ would have more burned-out missionaries than those making a powerful and positive impact on the world. Worse yet, innumerable missionaries would complete their callings and then live out their days in poverty.

> *Until pastors and leaders have a healthy and biblical outlook on finances, they will never be able to grow financially healthy churches.*

I told Carrie I had an idea I wanted to present to our board of trustees, which I did at our next meeting. At Grow Church we believe a safe, happy, and well-supported missionary can do much more on the mission field to benefit the kingdom of God than an unsupported missionary can; therefore, we are in support of meeting that missionary's needs. The board agreed to my proposal to sponsor the amount Carrie needed to return to the field, leaving her well supplied to do what God had called her to do. But that wasn't all God did for her.

I've learned God is interested in and capable of doing more than just one thing in our lives at a single time. Oftentimes, just when we think we understand something God has done for us, we look back and recognize He did a whole lot more than what we asked. And that is just where Carrie found herself in her situation.

When I next met with Carrie to discuss missional support and the increase in funding from Grow Church, Carrie learned that God never works on only one thing at a time and that He is always working for our good. Whereas Carrie had previously considered planning for her future as selfish, she realized doing so was not at all selfish. Not only was creating a deliberate budget a smart thing to do, but a budget that included *margin* was also necessary so that she could do what God had called her to do.

Of course, Carrie always understood God loves to support His people as they do what He has called them to do. But now she has a confident eye on her future because she has taken control of her finances in a way that will enable them to grow in a healthy manner throughout the coming years. She looks forward to the time when she will see Proverbs 13:22 fulfilled in her life: *A good person leaves an inheritance to their children's children* (NIV).

I want to be clear that Carrie was neither negligent nor irresponsible where finances were concerned. Like most people, she was never taught financial principles at school or in seminary and had no clue how to live a self-sufficient adult life. Living paycheck to paycheck is not God's best for His children, which is why we need to look at finances from God's perspective if we are to think strategically about the future. (This goes for both individuals and churches!)

You'll recall that helping people find freedom is part of our mission at Grow Church. Jesus said, *"And you shall know the truth, and the truth shall make you free"* (John 8:32). We know the Word of God is the only viable source of truth, so let's see how we can use its truths to establish a healthy outlook on finances.

You may be thinking, *"Pastor James, why are you spending so much time on these fundamental issues? Most people already know this."* No, they don't. I'm taking time to address this matter because until pastors and leaders have a healthy and biblical outlook on finances, they will never be able to grow financially healthy churches. A financially healthy church is led by financially healthy pastors, leaders, and staff members.

THE FINANCIAL BLAME GAME

> *People ruin their lives by their own foolishness and then are angry at the LORD* (PROVERBS 19:3 NLT).

One thing I've noticed about some Christians is that they are quick to praise God when things go well for them financially, but they also point the finger at Him when things don't go as they like. This financial blame game is not appropriate, because the Bible is clear that God is always looking out for us. In reality, those who play the blame game are unwilling to take the blame themselves for their own bad decisions or lack of knowledge and understanding.

God's Word is true, and it says, *His divine power has given to us all things that pertain to life and godliness, through the knowledge of Him who called us by glory and virtue, by which have been given to us exceedingly great and precious promises* (2 Peter 1:3–4). Sadly, far too many Christians are unwilling to put forth the effort to obtain the knowledge to master their financial conditions for the future. They may be fighting seemingly unsurmountable credit card debt, yet they incorrectly assume that if God wants them to have more money, He'll miraculously give it to them. Their poor decisions got them into a battle God never intended them to fight, yet He gets the blame for their being strapped to their pay checks month after month.

Understanding the truth about God's heart for finances, and wealth in general, is the first step in finding financial freedom. The Bible says, *But remember the LORD your God, for it is he who gives you the ability to produce wealth, and so confirms his covenant, which he swore to your ancestors, as it is today* (Deuteronomy 8:18 NIV). The Word also says, *A good person leaves an inheritance for their children's children, but a sinner's wealth is laid up for the righteous* (Proverbs 13:22 NIV). From these two verses we can assess God does not have a problem with our having money or even storing it up—so long as money doesn't become our god in place of Him.

Many people incorrectly cite the Bible as saying money is evil and that Christians are not supposed to have too much of it. But that's not what the Bible says. According to 1 Timothy 6:10, *For the love of money is a root of all kinds of evil. Some people, eager for money, have wandered from the faith and pierced themselves with many griefs* (NIV). Money is not the problem; rather, the *love* of money is what causes problems. If we love God first and foremost, then we can have money without money having us.

THE PRIORITIES OF MONEY

Moreover it is required in stewards that one be found faithful (1 CORINTHIANS 4:2).

A friend of mine with a large extended family once asked my advice on how to deal with some of his financially needy family members who continually asked him for money. His usual response was, "I don't have the funds right now," yet he felt as if he were lying to them.

He told me how God had blessed him and that he never wanted to be greedy or lack in generosity, yet some of his family members had the ability to make him feel bad about his success to the point he felt he was being taken advantage of. To help him gain a godly perspective on the matter, I started by asking these questions:

- Do you have a retirement account that makes you ready for retirement?

- Are you happy with the account, and could you retire today if you wanted to?

- Do you have a college fund for your kids that would enable them to attend college tomorrow without worries of running out of money?

- Have you started a fund that will help your kids prepare for their own retirement?

His answer to each of these questions was *no*, so I continued with other questions. At the end of our question-answer session, he realized that after exercising proper financial planning for his immediate future and that of his family's future, there wasn't a surplus of funds available to help those extended family members. He realized that when he told family members that he didn't have the money to help them he wasn't lying; instead, he now had a true understanding of his own financial position.

Oftentimes we need to reshape our understanding of our financial position so that our thoughts come in line with God's thoughts. Again, the Bible says, *A good person leaves an inheritance for their children's children* (Proverbs 13:22 NIV); therefore, we need to get to work to make this happen. God isn't going to simply create inheritance for us. To leave an inheritance requires our

At the core of every myth is always a corrupted biblical principle.

present-day stewardship of the money we now have; however, as we focus on the goal, God will add His favor to our efforts.

The true purpose of money is first to establish a sound financial base for our families and then to have the ability to extend a helping hand to others. The better we manage our money the more money comes our way. Jesus established this principle in His Parable of the Talents, in which He compared the kingdom of heaven to a man who entrusted his servants with talents (specific sums of money) for stewardship while he went on a journey. To one servant he gave five talents, to another servant two talents, and to the third one talent.

The servants who were given five and two talents both invested the talents and doubled their lord's money. But the third servant dug a hole and buried the talent entrusted to him. When the lord returned and saw that two of his servants had stewarded his money well, he commended them. But when the third servant merely returned his talent without gain, he said,

> "You wicked and lazy servant, you knew that I reap where I have not sown, and gather where I have not scattered seed. So you ought to have deposited my money with the bankers, and at my coming I would have received back my own with interest.
>
> "So take the talent from him, and give it to him who has ten talents. For to everyone who has, more will be given, and he will have abundance; but from him who does not have, even what he has will be taken away"
> (MATTHEW 25:26–29).

Clearly, God likes to reward those who do well with His money. The rich become richer because they understand the fundamental scriptural principles that govern money, yet many Christians don't take the time to learn these principles or practice them. Unbelievers use scriptural principles to become successful, while believers have these principles at their disposal but never take the time to obtain training in their use. This is the reason we offer a course in biblical prosperity at our Grow School of Ministry.

One of the topics I like to include in the course is that of myths and false religious traditions when it comes to money, some of which came from our good friend and overseer, Bishop Keith Butler of Word of Faith Ministries. Addressing the traditions of man, Jesus said, *"Thus you are nullifying and making void and of no effect [the authority of] the Word of God through your tra-dition, which you [in turn] hand on"* (Mark 7:13 AMPC).

Here are ten specific religious traditions concerning money that may have been passed down to us:

1. Money is the root of all evil; therefore, as committed Christians, we should not be concerned with savings or investments.

2. Poverty is a sign of spirituality.

3. It is wrong to build wealth and financial resources while here on earth.

4. All preachers want to get your money. The purpose of the local church is for worship of God, and it should stay out of people's business.

5. We will get our riches when we get to heaven.

6. If we really trust in Jesus and use our faith, He will meet all our financial needs without our having to do anything about our circumstances.

7. God answers prayer; therefore, we don't need to plan ahead. If we will pray and take one day at a time, God will take care of us. We don't need to make preparation for the future.

8. God is interested only in spiritual matters, not the mundane material concerns of everyday life.

9. Money is corrupt, and it will lead us astray. If a person has money, he or she must be stealing it from someone else.

10. When an individual tithes, God is automatically bound to meet all his or her financial needs without that person's adherence to the principles that govern money as outlined in the Bible.

At the core of every myth is always a corrupted biblical principle; therefore, many of our attitudes about God's provision are distorted because of misinformation. These and other religious traditions are responsible for robbing believers of our economic inheritance.

We counter these myths, traditions, and corrupted principles first by renewing our minds with the Word of God: *And do not be conformed to this world, but be transformed by the renewing of your mind, that you may prove what is that good and acceptable and perfect will of God* (Romans 12:2). Then we actively and deliberately replace religious tradition with God's truth by *casting down arguments and every high thing that exalts itself against the knowledge of God, bringing every thought captive to the obedience of Christ* (2 Corinthians 10:5).

Jesus said, *"You cannot serve both God and money"* (Matthew 6:24 NIV). We are not to serve money; rather, money is to be our servant. It is a form of blessing in our hands so that we can, in turn, be a blessing to others.

THE BLESSING OF OBEDIENCE

> *If you fully obey the LORD your God and carefully follow all his commandments I give you today, the LORD your God will set you high above all the nations on earth* (DEUTERONOMY 28:1 NIV).

Natural acts determine spiritual benefits. What I mean by this simple statement is that God doesn't bless us without reason, as we can see in Genesis 1 when He established His blessing in the beginning:

> Then God said, "Let Us make man in Our image, according to Our likeness; let them have dominion ..." So God created man in His own image; in the image of God He created him; male and female He created them. Then God blessed them, and God said to them, "Be fruitful and multiply; fill the earth and subdue it; have dominion over the fish of the sea, over the birds of the air, and over every living thing that moves on the earth" (GENESIS 1:26–28).

God intended mankind to experience a life of continual blessing, but we know our original ancestors essentially "blew it" when they disobeyed the one command He'd given them: *"Of every tree of the garden you may freely eat; but of the tree of the knowledge of good and evil you shall not eat"* (Genesis 2:16–17). Adam and Eve's act of disobedience determined their spiritual benefits or, in this case, their loss of benefits, in that they were expelled from the garden.

But when, through Moses, God established His covenant with His people, we again see His blessing demonstrated in every imaginable way—as detailed in Deuteronomy 8:3–13—so long as the people obeyed His voice.

When we choose to align ourselves in obedience with God's Word, His purpose, and His calling, then we will experience the benefits of His blessing in our lives. When it comes to money and finances, if we steward them according to His principles, then God shows up and blesses our efforts. If we choose not to steward according to His principles, then He is not obligated to bless us. God will indeed provide for our needs, but if we want His blessing on our lives beyond our needs, we need to open the door for Him through our obedience.

Obedience to biblical financial principles is not merely a New Testament precept. We see it in the Old Testament as well. I especially like this story from the book of 1 Kings about a widow who met the prophet Elijah during a time of severe drought in the land. Elijah asked her to bring him a cup of water.

> And as she was going to get it, he called to her and said, "Please bring me a morsel of bread in your hand."
>
> So she said, "As the LORD your God lives, I do not have bread, only a handful of flour in a bin, and a little oil in a jar; and see, I am gathering a couple of sticks that I may go in and prepare it for myself and my son, that we may eat it, and die."

And Elijah said to her, "Do not fear; go and do as you have said, but make me a small cake from it first, and bring it to me; and afterward make some for yourself and your son. For thus says the LORD God of Israel: 'The bin of flour shall not be used up, nor shall the jar of oil run dry, until the day the LORD sends rain on the earth.'"

So she went away and did according to the word of Elijah; and she and he and her household ate for many days. The bin of flour was not used up, nor did the jar of oil run dry, according to the word of the LORD which He spoke by Elijah (1 KINGS 17:11–16).

Because of this woman's obedience to the word from God, spoken through Elijah, her needs were met, and she had no lack. God loves all who have received Jesus as Savior and Lord unconditionally, whether we choose to act on His principles or we don't. His blessing is available for us through our obedience to His Word and His principles; however, when we abide in His Word wholeheartedly, we see His favor come upon us in amazing ways.

An integral correlation exists between skillful money management (stewardship) and spiritual benefits (blessings). Far too many Christian families wander aimlessly through life without ever realizing the godly significance attached to material possessions. If our financial houses are not in order, we cannot be a blessing to others. Jesus affirms this truth with His teachings:

- *And he said to him, "Well done, good servant;
  because you were faithful in a very little, have
  authority over ten cities" (Luke 19:17).*

- *"Therefore if you have not been faithful in the
  unrighteous mammon, who will commit to
  your trust the true riches?" (Luke 16:11).*

- *"His lord said to him, 'Well done, good and faithful
  servant; you were faithful over a few things, I
  will make you ruler over many things. Enter into
  the joy of your lord'" (Matthew 25:21).*

Remember, natural acts—whether of obedience or disobedience—determine spiritual blessings. Let's choose the blessing of obedience, for out of it comes a healthy outlook on finances. And only when we have a healthy—and biblical—outlook on finances, are we able to move forward in growing a healthy church.

CHAPTER SIX REVIEW:

1. Retirement, savings, college funds, and emergency funds (to name a few) are vital for an individual's future success. It is not selfish to focus on these and other financial tools, even when you're in ministry.

   » **CHALLENGE:** Consider communicating about personal finances with your staff quarterly to keep healthy concepts in front of them, while working toward a benefit package that helps them achieve their financial goals for the future.

2. If you do not have a savings or retirement account setup for yourself, then you do not yet have additional funds for other initiatives.

   » **CHALLENGE:** This seems like a selfish request, but if you are not prepared for the future, you will find yourself stressed and over-burdened in the future. Consider getting these two accounts started in your life, and then help you staff get there as well.

3. There are plenty of lies about money, which many believers think are truths.

   » **CHALLENGE:** Take your staff through the religious traditions concerning money portion of this chapter to help them think differently about money.

4. Obedience is the surest way to encounter the blessing of God.

   » **CHALLENGE:** Consider communicating to your staff what obedience in stewardship looks like according to the Word of God. Doing so will create a simple shift in their financial outlook that will springboard them into the blessing and favor of God.

_____

_____

_____

_____

CHAPTER SEVEN

BIBLICAL STEWARDSHIP: HERE'S HOW IT LOOKS

"The surplus wealth we have gained to some extent at least belongs to our fellow beings; we are only the temporary custodians of our fortunes, and let us be careful that no just complaint can be made against our stewardship." —JACOB SCHIFF

"The one principle that surrounds everything else is that of stewardship; that we are the managers of everything that God has given us." —LARRY BURKETT

"There can be no stewardship without stewards." —JOHN JAY JACKSON, JR.

"Don't tell me you're trusting God until you trust Him with your pocketbook." —J. VERNON MCGEE

The average American family goes in the hole on a continual basis because family members spend more than they make—and they don't even realize it.

Most people, including Christians, have at least one credit card they've been trying to pay off for years. The credit card companies get richer and richer, while Christians become poorer and poorer. Jesus said, *"He who is faithful in what is least is faithful also in much; and he who is unjust in what is least is unjust also in much"* (Luke 16:10). Here's the James Boyd translation of this Bible verse: Be faithful with what you have, starting where you are. As you demonstrate your faithfulness with small amounts of money, God will give you more. If you don't properly manage a small income, you won't be able to manage a larger income.

> *Remember, obedience to God's Word and His principles always brings blessing.*

In case you're wondering, I'm still focusing on financial fundamentals, because without them we cannot build financially healthy churches.

Biblical stewardship is the key to success with God. There is a practical way to be good and faithful stewards as the Word calls us to be, a principle I first learned from Andy Stanley as the Give-Save-Live principle. Simply stated, starting with the income we have to work with, the principle says we should first *give*, then *save*, and finally *live*. In that order. You'll recall that helping people find freedom is part of our mission at Grow Church, and financial freedom is something we value highly—so much so, that we've adopted Andy Stanley's Give-Save-Live principle as our own.

If we can live according to this principle—which we can do with deliberate stewardship—we will eliminate virtually all financial stress. We will honor God. We will have healthy marriages (most marriage troubles are the result of not having finances in order), and we will be genuinely happier.

The following chart illustrates the Give-Save-Live principle on both a personal basis as well as how it looks at Grow Church:

EXPENSES

	PERSONAL	GROW CHURCH
GIVE	Tithe	Missions
	Offering	Over-and-Above Giving
	Talents & Serving	Community Serve Events
SAVE	Emergency Fund	Six-Month Reserve
	Retirement	401k Match
	College Fund	Endowment
LIVE	Needs	Utilities, Staffing, Insurance, etc.
	Wants	Advancement Investments

Now, on the following page, let's break down each component of the Give-Save-Live chart.

The *Give* component is, of course, the tithe. In biblical terms the tithe is the first fruits, or the top 10 percent, off the gross amount of income, prior to taxes. I know of Christians who believe tithing is an Old Testament principle and that as New Testament believers they are to be givers of offerings only. I never argue their point; rather, I continue to reap the blessings that come from both tithing *and* giving offerings. I don't expect God will ever come to me and say, "James, I sure could have blessed you more if only you'd given less." The bottom line is this: giving should always be the number-one priority for every believer as well as for every church. The saying "You can't outgive God!" is certainly true.

The *Save* component ensures we will have funds to satisfy any emergency needs that may arise unexpectedly—and they *will* arise. However, when we properly steward the finances we've been given and God's blessings increase, we'll have less need for those emergency funds, which can then be invested. Saved money is what we lean on when we have a need, but invested money grows. By saving and investing money, we are investing in our future—and our future thanks us for that.

The *Live* component is both the most important and least important component of this stewardship principle. The *Live* component represents expenses. If we give and save, then God will involve Himself in the *Live* component—whether in our personal finances or in the church's finances. Remember, obedience to God's Word and His principles always brings blessing. And the point of our being blessed is that we may first take care of our families and then have enough left to help others.

ESTABLISH A BUDGET

> *"For which of you, intending to build a tower, does not sit down first and count the cost, whether he has enough to finish it—lest, after he has laid the foundation, and is not able to finish, all who see it begin to mock him, saying, 'This man began to build and was not able to finish'?"* (LUKE 14:28–30).

In the day in which we live, biblical stewardship on a personal level begins with a personal budget. Tracy and I have always maintained a personal budget, and we encourage our staff to do the same. According to personal finance advisor Dave Ramsey, "A budget is telling your money where to go instead of wondering where it went."

On the following two pages are a sample personal budget for a single individual and a monthly tracking chart to reconcile actual numbers and budgeted numbers.

At the top of the budget are the *income* lines detailing the total *take-home* income each month. Total take-home income would include the net paycheck for those who have jobs, as well as any freelance work or other income.

Next are the *expenses* lines, prioritized beginning with giving, savings, emergency margin, and retirement. Though these items are not considered expenses in the true sense of the word, it's helpful to include them to have a true overall picture of finances and to ensure that all needs are comfortably met each month.

PERSONAL BUDGET SAMPLE

INCOME		MONTHLY
Salary		$6,000
Freelance		1,000
Other Income		200
TOTAL INCOME		**$7,200**

EXPENSES	NOTES	MONTHLY
Giving—Tithe/Offering	of Gross not Net	$720
Savings	10%	720
Emergency Margin	2%	144
Retirement	3% + matching	216
Income Taxes	35% guestimate	2,520
Rent		1,500
Holiday/Friends gifts		70
Travel		
Food	(7-day trip x 3 annually)	70
Flights	(3 trips annually)	85
Beauty		50
Shopping		50
Restaurant/Food		40
Coffee		20
Activities/Entertainment		50
Toiletries		50
Groceries		200
Dues/Subscriptions		20
Car		
Maintenance		20
Car Wash		5
Oil		15
Fuel		130
Insurance		200
Medical/Doctor		75
Health Insurance	Company participates	150
TOTAL EXPENSE		**$7,120**
INCOME AFTER EXPENSE		**$80**

MONTHLY TRACKING
(throughout the year)

INCOME	JANUARY	FEBRUARY	MARCH
Salary			
Freelance			
Other Income			
TOTAL INCOME			

EXPENSES			
Giving—Tithe/Offering			
Savings			
Emergency Margin			
Retirement			
Income Taxes			
Rent			
Holiday/Friends Gifts			
Travel			
Food			
Flights			
Beauty			
Shopping			
Restaurant/Food			
Coffee			
Activities/Entertainment			
Toiletries			
Groceries			
Dues/Subscriptions			
Car			
Maintenance			
Car Wash			
Oil			
Fuel			
Insurance			
Medical/Doctor			
Health Insurance			
TOTAL EXPENSE			
NET INCOME			

Again, establishing a personal budget is a form of biblical stewardship. For those who have never established a budget, I recommend starting with the simple chart above and then customizing it. Afterward, it's good to have a trusted individual look over the budget to confirm it is realistic and accomplishable.

The next step is to track progress on the *Monthly Tracking* chart by reconciling actual numbers and budgeted numbers. The literal meaning of the word *reconcile* is "to bring into agreement or harmony." For instance, let's say a friend named Barb has a budgeted income of $2,900 per month but one month she earned $500 in freelance work, so her total income would be $3,400. Likewise with expenses: if Barb had an unexpected medical expense, then her total expenses would increase. (However, if Barb has been faithful to put money in savings each month, that expense should be covered.)

One thing I've seen happen over and again is that once people get the hang of stewarding their finances, they never want to go back to the way they lived. Tracking actual income and expenses on a monthly basis puts people in control, not only of their finances, but also of life in general. The reason stewarding God's way works so well is that people have put God in control by putting Him first when they tithe and give offerings. When we put God first in our finances, He sees to it that we are blessed. According to the Word of God, *The blessing of the LORD makes one rich, and He adds no sorrow with it* (Proverbs 10:22). God blesses those who give to others, because His return on that investment always comes in the form of increased blessing to His bride, the Church.

ESTABLISH A HEALTHY FINANCIAL GOAL

The plans of the diligent lead to profit as surely as haste leads to poverty (PROVERBS 21:5 NIV).

The goal of the Give-Save-Live principle of biblical stewardship is for individuals to live within 80 percent of their income. I've always had a personal goal to live at under 50 percent. Of course, I didn't start at that number; however, through faithful steward-ship of my finances I got there.

To live within 80 percent of one's income is to *give* 10 percent, *save* 10 percent, and *live* on 80 percent. People who have adopted the Give-Save-Live principle have often said something like this to me: "Pastor James, I can't tell you how much stress I've elim-inated from my life and how much joy has come in its place!" They tell me they sleep better at night and are more motivated and energized. That's because they've gained the financial control they were always intended to have but just didn't know it.

This is what establishing a healthy financial goal will do for anyone willing to make the commitment and stick to it.

DEBT: FRIEND OR FOE?

Let no debt remain outstanding (ROMANS 13:8 NIV).

Many years ago when I was in college, I attended a party at the home of my then-girlfriend, whose parents were hosting a group of her father's business associates and had invited us to join them. On our way to the house, my friend and I were discussing finances, a topic I was already interested in, and I remember her telling me her parents were in debt about $150,000, and under a lot of pressure. She also said the situation had put stress on their relationship.

Debt causes worry, anxiety, and conflict with family and friends.

When we arrived, I could see that her parents had gone all out for this party—it was awesome; however, I couldn't get our conversation about their finances out of my mind. By the looks of things, the cost of that party must have taken them $10-$15,000 further into debt. Even as a college student with only a basic understanding of budgeting, finances, and debt, I could see they were in trouble.

Sadly, far too many people have had absolutely *no* training in these critical matters that pertain to living a godly and successful life. Here are a few things I've learned about debt, which I often share when helping others:

- When debt gets out of control, it renders people useless to the kingdom.

- Debt becomes one's master.

- Debt weakens family foundations.

- Debt comes as a result of greed or lack of self-control.

- Debt is usually a result of poor planning or no planning at all.

- Debt is a thief that robs.

- Debt causes worry, anxiety, and conflict with family and friends.

- Debt destroys our Christian witness and prevents us from being a blessing.

- Debt requires a transfer of wealth from the borrower to the lender.

- Debt makes a presumption on the future, which means you're paying now for something that you *believe* you can afford later.

- Debt is a curse.

We should pay off all credit-card debt monthly. If we cannot do so, then we should not trust ourselves with any type of debit or credit cards. I've had only one month in my life that I didn't pay off my entire credit-card balance, and I didn't sleep well for the next thirty days. I promised myself I would never do that again, and it's a promise I've kept for more than twenty years now.

When I'm asked if all debt is bad, my immediate answer is *no*, but then I go on to explain. Some debt is okay, but it should be in context of *loan to value*. The loan-to-value ratio is a figure that lenders use to determine how much risk they have on a secured loan, which measures the relationship between the loan amount and the market value of the property. For example, let's say Joe and Mary own a home valued at $400,000, but they owe the bank $350,000. Though they have $50,000 in equity, they are not in a safe position because markets could shift and quickly put them in an upside-down position (meaning the value of their house could

Vehicles lose value, so they are not assets, but rather liabilities.

decrease to the point they owe more than it's worth). I recommend a maximum 50 percent loan-to-value ratio when buying a home. If the home is valued at $400,000, then the loan should be no greater than $200,000. This ratio can be hard to accomplish but it is a valid goal.

Here's an interesting fact: home loans are cheap money because interest rates are generally the lowest on a personal residence; however, credit-card debt is expensive—sometimes as much as 25 percent in the interest arena. Yikes!

When it comes to buying a vehicle, paying cash is always optimal. But for those who can't yet pay cash and need to secure a loan, use the same 50 percent *loan-to-value* approach as when buying a home. In other words, the car's value should be double what is owed on it. To accomplish this means paying half the price of the vehicle in cash (which requires advance planning) or finding an amazing deal.

Vehicle debt is generally expensive debt. Most people think their vehicle is a symbol of their prosperity, but it's many times a symbol of a lack of stewardship. Vehicles lose value, so they are not assets, but rather liabilities. I often tell people that the more money they spend on a vehicle the more money they are okay with losing. Vehicles are never a good investment, so it's always best to drive one that's below our means and worth double what is owed on it. This is how we stay safe where debt is concerned.

STEWARDSHIP IS HARD WORK

You will eat the fruit of your labor; blessings and prosperity will be yours (PSALMS 128:2 NIV).

You likely now know I'm a big proponent of up-front, hard work. Little wonder one of my favorite books is *Do Hard Things: A Teenage Rebellion* by Alex and Brett Harris. Published in 2016, the book ignited a movement in young people to rebel against our culture's low expectations for them and instead fulfill God's long-term plans. Written for students, its truths are equally applicable for adults.

Though most people no longer believe that doing the hard things in life comes with an inevitable, big payoff, the principle is still true. My motto is this: "If doing something isn't hard, it's likely not worth doing!" Stewardship in finances is what keeps us from hurts in the future. I'm oftentimes so engaged in the process of hard work that I must challenge myself to slow down enough so that I can hear from God. I'd rather err on the side of action as opposed to being complacent. The way I see it, faith is an action word, and I want to be on the move in my life so that I'm always ready to walk through the doors God opens for me. This is the reason why it's crucial we do our future a favor and get our finances in order—both personal finances and church finances.

We established a benevolence process at Grow Church to help people in need; however, this process is not intended to merely meet a current need but also to teach people how to help themselves as they move forward. The first step is the application process that enables us to fully understand the request. Next, we have an initial meeting with the applicants to look at their giving history as well as their income and expenses. Those in need typically do not have a good giving history, so we help them determine how they can cut expenses, lower payments, and eliminate some expense items altogether.

Sadly, most people have a hard time accepting the idea they can live without cable TV or their Starbuck's coffee that costs them $2,500 annually. Getting finances in order is no joke, which means there is usually a season of sacrifice people will go through. But it is during this season we show God we are serious about His financial management system and that we trust Him.

Those who are willing to do the up-front, hard work to establish godly stewardship will always experience God's grace throughout the process. And the good news is that the hard work becomes easy once finances are set up correctly.

Below are some of my favorite Bible verses pertaining to the rewards of sound biblical stewardship:

- *Lazy hands make for poverty, but diligent hands bring wealth* (Proverbs 10:4 NIV).

- *Diligent hands will rule, but laziness ends in forced labor* (Proverbs 12:24 NIV).

- *The lazy do not roast any game, but the diligent feed on the riches of the hunt* (Proverbs 12:27 NIV).

- *A sluggard's appetite is never filled, but the desires of the diligent are fully satisfied* (Proverbs 13:4 NIV).

- *The plans of the diligent lead to profit as surely as haste leads to poverty* (Proverbs 21:5 NIV).

And let me just add my own James Boyd proverb to this list: God rewards those who are diligent with their finances!

1. Give, Save, Live—These are the three ingredients to stress free, God-honoring living.

   » **CHALLENGE:** Put together a personal budget with these three ingredients evident in it. This budget will be a starting point that you can share with your staff (after removing your personal numbers, of course) to help them grow in their financial life.

2. Monthly budget reconciliations are key to stay on track for your bigger goals.

   » **CHALLENGE:** If you're not in the habit of reconciling your budget each month, now is a great time to start. Staying on target with your budget will become increasingly more important for you personally and for your organization because it will keep you on financial track as you grow.

3. Debt weakens families and organizations.

   » **CHALLENGE:** Create a plan to go debt free, or to minimize your debt, and work the plan.

4. Doing hard things pays off.

   » **CHALLENGE:** Put together a play book of the hard things you want to do this year to find success in your initiatives.

_____

_____

_____

_____

_____

_____

_____

_____

PART TWO

DOING THE WORK OF MINISTRY

Whatever may be your task, work at it heartily (from the soul), as [something done] for the Lord and not for men, knowing [with all certainty] that it is from the Lord [and not from men] that you will receive the inheritance that is your [real] reward.

—COLOSSIANS 3:23–24 AMPC

HOW TO SET AND MEASURE GOALS

"Someone's sitting in the shade today because someone planted a tree a long time ago." —WARREN BUFFETT

"Opportunities are usually disguised as hard work, so most people don't recognize them." —ANN LANDERS

"Entrepreneurs are simply those who understand that there is little difference between obstacle and opportunity and are able to turn both to their advantage." —VICTOR KIAM

"A pessimist sees the difficulty in every opportunity; an optimist sees the opportunity in every difficulty." —WINSTON S. CHURCHILL

One of the most revealing and helpful books I read in the early days of leadership at Grow Church was titled *The 4 Disciplines of Execution* by Chris McChesney, Sean Covey, and Jim Huling. The promotional copy on the back cover of the book boldly declared that by adhering to the proven practices detailed within its pages, we could expect breakthrough results in achieving our most important goals and priorities. After reading the back cover, I was sold. I proceeded to devour the book, after which the staff and I established at Grow Church some of the book's concepts from the four disciplines because we believed we would see results if we stuck to the guided steps.

Our experience in setting and measuring goals was based on the four disciplines outlined in the book:

- Focus on the wildly important goal (WIG)
- Act on the lead measures
- Keep a compelling scorecard
- Create a cadence of accountability

FOCUS ON THE WILDLY IMPORTANT GOAL (WIG)

I press on toward the goal to win the [supreme and heavenly] prize to which God in Christ Jesus is calling us upward (PHILIPPIANS 3:14 AMPC).

The premise of this discipline requires a pastor or leader to go against his or her leadership instincts to focus on *less* so that the staff can achieve *more*.

Instead of working to make significant improvements in everything all at once, focus on the number-one, most-important goal—the *wildly important goal,* the WIG. Most organizations get so caught up in their day-to-day operations and tasks, they forget about their big goals they intended to achieve and that they built their staffs to meet. Make it clear to the staff that the WIG is the goal that matters most and that failure to achieve this big goal will make every other achievement seem inconsequential.

Oftentimes, when I'm asked to evaluate the efficacy of a church, leaders are surprised at the number of endeavors their staffs are engaged in—most all of them good—that fall outside the original purpose and calling of their churches.

An organization that has anywhere from five to twenty goals makes it virtually impossible for the staff to maintain focus. By narrowing the focus to one (or possibly two) wildly important goals, staff members can easily distinguish what is truly top priority. I personally believe that where the local church is concerned, establishing the *wildly important goal* is something the staff should be involved in, rather than its being determined solely by the pastor. When staff members are involved, they will wholeheartedly participate in achieving the goal.

ACT ON THE LEAD MEASURES

Then I raised my eyes and looked, and behold, a man with a measuring line in his hand (ZECHARIAH 2:1).

The progress and success of any strategy will be based on two kinds of measures: lag measures and lead measures. The business world knows these measures as KPIs, or key performance indicators. These KPIs guide a staff toward the vision of the organization.

The simplest definition of the word *lag* is "to stay behind"; therefore, a *lag measure* is a measure of performance of an event or occurrence that has already taken place. Let's say, for instance, that a recording artist agrees to perform at a benefit concert for a particular charity. The day after the performance, organizers report that ten thousand people purchased tickets at $20 each, grossing $200,000 for the charity. The number of people who attended the event and the amount of money raised are lag measures; the performance that drove those numbers is already in the past.

Lead measures are the high-impact activities or strategies you and your staff must accomplish to reach your goal. They measure the new behaviors that must be established to drive success on the lag measures.

To understand the relationship between lead and lag measures, let's examine them in the context of a goal of losing weight: The lag measure would be the number of pounds lost, while two lead measures might be a set caloric intake and a specific number of exercise minutes each day. Lead measures are predictive in that, by performing them, you can predict the lag measure the bathroom scale will give you at the end of the week.

KEEP A COMPELLING SCORECARD

But you shall have a perfect and just weight and
a perfect and just measure, that your days may
be prolonged in the land which the LORD your
God gives you (DEUTERONOMY 25:15 AMPC).

In the world of sports, the highest level of performance comes from athletes who are emotionally engaged with their team as they work toward the common goal of winning the game. The highest level of their engagement comes from their knowing the game score, whether they are winning or losing.

In applying this discipline of scorecard keeping in the non-sports world, we've found the kind of scorecard that drives the highest level of engagement of a business or church staff is one designed solely for—and oftentimes by—the staff. It is also a scorecard that enables staff members to keep score.

A clear scorecard keeps the staff engaged with the goal and greatly reduces the likelihood of their abandoning that goal for other pressing activities. Any staff members who don't know if they are winning or losing are probably on the way to losing.

CREATE A CADENCE OF ACCOUNTABILITY

Nothing in all creation is hidden from God's sight.
Everything is uncovered and laid bare before the eyes of
him to whom we must give account (HEBREWS 4:13 NIV).

The *cadence of accountability* is a rhythm of frequent and regular meetings of any staff working toward a wildly important goal. Accountability should always begin with the leadership of the organization and include every staff member, from top to bottom. Accountability brings encouragement to others and keeps the organization on track.

Accountability meetings should occur weekly and last between twenty and thirty minutes, during which time staff members should hold each other accountable for producing results.

Establishing a repeated cadence allows staff members to create their own commitments to getting results. People will always be more committed to their own ideas than they will be to taking orders from someone else. By making commitments to fellow staff members, the relational emphasis shifts from professional to personal.

When fully engaged staff members, functioning comfortably in a cadence of accountability, see the lag measure of a wildly important goal moving as a direct result of their efforts, they know they are winning. And nothing drives staff morale and engagement more than winning.

———

Armed with the knowledge we'd gleaned from *The 4 Disciplines of Execution,* Tracy and I were ready to meet with the Grow Church staff to establish our very first WIG. We initially assessed our wildly important goal to be growing our weekend attendance, but shortly after we'd made that determination, it didn't sit well with us. We realized that if the leadership team did not expand at the same rate as attendance, then we wouldn't be able to keep up with the growth. So we pulled the staff together again and reevaluated our position.

We had a lot of new people visiting each weekend, but we knew that if we couldn't tighten up our discipleship process to develop fully devoted followers of Jesus, we wouldn't have an adequate pool of people necessary to support the growth. Another book that provided much-needed direction at that time was *Traction: Get a Grip on Your Business* by Gino Wickman. The book challenged us to think about the one system we could count on to continue to grow our church, to be our wildly important goal. For Grow Church, that system was our discipleship process, which began with Grow Steps, a two-step procedure that (1) helps each person discover his or her God-given gifts and (2) shows them how to use those gifts to fulfill the purpose God created them to fulfill.

The two most significant tools we use to help people during the Grow Steps process are the *DiSC®* profile and our Spiritual Gifts Assessment tools.

DiSC® is an acronym that represents the four main personality profiles: dominance, influence, steadiness, and conscientiousness. When individuals understand how they respond to conflict, what motivates them or causes stress, and how they respond to problems, they can be more effective in both their personal lives and their working situations, whether business or ministry.

For instance, people with "D" personalities tend to be confident, and they value accomplishing bottom-line results. Those with "I" personalities place an emphasis on relationships and influencing or persuading others. "S" personalities tend to be dependable, cooperative, and sincere, while "C" personalities emphasize quality, accuracy, expertise, and competency.

Our Spiritual Gifts Assessment tool, obtained from Church of the Highlands, enables us to guide people in a personal discovery of their spiritual gifts that are found in scripture in 1 Corinthians 12. This assessment is a very important tool to us, for we consider Grow Church a gifts-based church, not a needs-based church. What this means is that we have positioned the church to help people find their purpose and serve in an area that expands them personally toward their calling. We do not ask anyone to serve where we have the greatest need at the current time. Grow Church is set in this community to guide people in their walk with God and focus on themselves first, instead of focusing on the church's needs first. We have found this assessment enlightens people and helps them plug into a culture of next steps in their development. *DiSC®* and the Spiritual Gifts Assessment tool combined are a dynamic mixture that serves people in their journey with Jesus.

Grow Steps is the gateway through which come the future volunteers and leaders necessary to support the growth of the church. Once we established Grow Steps as our WIG, the next question was how to determine the number of volunteers and leaders we would need. We made that determination by what I refer to as the *10-3-1 Process* for setting goals.

THE 10-3-1 PROCESS

Then the LORD answered me and said, "Write the vision and make it plain" (HABAKKUK 2:2).

The *10-3-1 Process* represents ten-year goals, three-year goals, and one-year goals—established in that order.

At the time, our ten-year goal for Grow Church was an attendance of five thousand people, with five locations in our immediate area. As we focused on leadership development rather than attendance numbers, we knew the *10-3-1 Process* would ensure that our Grow Steps discipleship process was a success. Starting with the ten-year goal, we first calculated the number of people we'd need to develop into leaders and to serve as volunteers to care for five thousand people at five locations.

Not all church systems operate in the same way; however, on the basis of our numbers at the time, we knew it took five hundred people on the combined leadership- and volunteer-serving teams to accommodate a weekend attendance of fifteen hundred people. This number of volunteers may seem high to some, but at Grow Church we lean toward the concept of "the more people serving, the better." We've found that with this 30 percent ratio of volunteers, every first-time visitor gets an average of seven to ten personal connections before he or she leaves the building.

Looking ahead to our ten-year goal of five thousand people in five locations, at a ratio of 30 percent volunteers, we would need sixteen hundred people trained and ready to lead and serve. To get the three-year goal numbers, we simply multiplied the ten-year numbers by 33.3 percent and then, to get the one-year goal numbers, we multiplied the three-year numbers by 33.3 percent. We felt good when we saw that our one-year goal numbers were larger than our present numbers, which meant that, with a little bit of God's grace and a whole lot of work, we could accomplish that first goal.

We also had to factor in the goal of having four additional locations within the ten-year period, which meant launching a new location approximately every two years. If our broadcast location continued to accommodate 1,500 people, and each new location had an attendance of 875 people, we'd need to have about 270 volunteers ready to serve at each additional location. Of course, those volunteers would not serve at every service. Most would serve once each month, with some preferring to serve two to four times monthly.

WORKING THE WIG

Roll your works upon the Lord [commit and trust them wholly to Him] ... so shall your plans be established and succeed (PROVERBS 16:3 AMPC).

With our Grow Steps discipleship process firmly established as our WIG, and our *10-3-1 Process* goal numbers in place, we next needed to calculate the required number of people to complete the Grow Steps process each month and then successfully connect to the right serving team to add 270 new volunteers every two years.

While the goal of adding a new campus in two years was excit-ing, of greater importance were the 270 new people who would be fulfilling their purpose in the kingdom of God as they became fully developed followers of Christ. That was (and is) the result we want to obtain; however, to obtain this result the church must grow, and our job is to prepare for that growth.

An average of forty people completed the Grow Steps process each month, and of that number 25 percent of them connected with the right serving team and continued to serve. That meant we added a solid ten people per month to our two-year goal of 270. We knew it was *possible* to complete the mission with 240, but that number wasn't optimal; therefore, we took the opportu-nity before us to determine practical ways to increase both the number of people going through the Grow Steps process as well as our retention rate. Identifying an issue is always the first step in resolving the issue.

Again, it is vital the staff be involved in goal setting, and espe-cially so for our directors since they are in charge of the various departments within the church. Directors are the ones responsi-ble for building their teams of volunteers, which puts them in the best place to determine and set their departmental wildly import-ant goals. When staff members determine the method (or lead measure) to accomplish their goals, they have complete buy-in ownership of the process. They also have complete trust in the Grow Steps process they are guiding people to.

SETTING DEPARTMENTAL MEASURES

*Many are the plans in a person's heart, but it is the
LORD's purpose that prevails* (PROVERBS 19:21 NIV).

Each of our department directors submitted his or her own plans
for approval, but since most all churches have a children's ministry, I'll use the plan submitted by our Grow Kids director to
demonstrate how the process worked for us. Remember, Grow
Church's wildly important goal is to increase the number of people going through the Grow Steps discipleship process.

Grow Kids thrives because of the volunteers who serve faith-
fully in that ministry; therefore, we need a constant flow of people
coming through Grow Steps and into Grow Kids. We've learned
that the best way to present Grow Steps to people is through
relationship building (regardless of which department they later
choose to serve in). After all, when you trust someone, you'll
allow them to take you on a journey.

Relationship-building activities can be as simple as meeting
for a cup of coffee or fresh brewed tea. So how many meetings
with new families—or those not yet plugged into serving—does
it take to meet the Grow Kids ministry goals of team growth? For
our church we determined that number to be five per week to
build and sustain the growth of the volunteer team (each department determined its own WIG numbers). We also knew, based
on experience, that it took extending ten invitations to get five
confirmed in-person connections with families. This meant the
weekly lag measures for Grow Kids was ten invitations and five

meetings with a lead member of the ministry. The monthly lag measures were forty and twenty respectively.

Invitations could be extended in numerous ways. For instance, a great time for the Grow Kids director to connect with families was during the Sunday morning check-in process. Of course, it's not possible for her to connect with everyone, so oftentimes she would write a personal note of invitation to a family and have one of the volunteers deliver it. Extending an invitation in this manner ensured that the entire team was contributing to the success of the department in developing leaders.

Another lag measure was the training a volunteer received after completing the Grow Steps process. Potential new team members shadow one of the lead Grow Kids team members during a Sunday service to review the role and determine if it is a good fit.

These are just two examples of how departmental lag measures can be managed and then land on the monthly scorecard. Now let's look at lead measures.

Remember, lead measures are the high-impact activities or strategies that you and your staff must accomplish to reach your goal. They measure the new behaviors that drive success on the lag measures. Lead measures help the staff members and volunteers stay on focus to develop people, create relationships, and build up others for the benefit of the body of Christ. At Grow Church, we have four lead measures that are applicable to every department. They are the (1) ask, (2) train, (3) transfer, and (4) one-on-one.

The *ask* is the official invitation to join a volunteer team. This happens after an individual has completed the Grow Steps discipleship process and is approved to join a team. Some people are ready to join a team immediately after completing the process, others prefer to take their time to be sure they are a good fit for the team. Either way, nothing happens without the ask.

The *train* is for those who want to join a team, but they need training. Proper training is vital to successful and fulfilling ministry, and it is an integral part of the team-building process at Grow Church. People who are fulfilled in their roles within the church keep the church healthy.

The *transfer* occurs when one person ministers to another, giving them a spiritual impartation. For instance, if a team member is seeking God's will in a particular personal situation and asks for prayer, the one praying might offer a prayer of impartation according to James 1:5: *If any of you lacks wisdom, let him ask of God ... and it will be given to him.*

The *one-on-one* is the personal time we spend getting to know a person, connecting with him or her, and sharing our hearts with each other. This is where strong, godly relationships are forged.

These four common lead measures allow the directors of each department to ensure people are being taken through a process of personal growth as they become connected with their respective volunteer teams.

We have seen this process work well in the past year. Whereas we had previously struggled to find volunteers that felt purpose in the children's department, after about six to eight months of keeping these disciplines in place and accountable via scorecard, we noticed a fully energetic volunteer team with enough people to back up positions when life's circumstances got in the way.

It was good that we started measuring results and keeping the process accountable, because during implementation we started planning for a second location launch. As you probably know, a second location would not be possible without a reproducible system of building teams. Thank God He started pointing us in this direction when He did; if not, we would have had to hold up what He was asking us to do in starting an additional location. This process is similar to the margin concept: preparing for what God wants to do so that we're ready when He wants to do it.

CHAPTER EIGHT REVIEW:

1. Wildly important goals help keep members of an organization focused together on the most important thing.

   » **CHALLENGE:** Consider what your WIG is for your organization. After you have a good idea of what it is, pull together three-to-five staff members to evaluate it with you. Then, communicate your WIG to your staff as the focus for the year.

2. Lag measures, lead measures, and a scorecard will help guide your success.

   » **CHALLENGE:** Set some lag measures that can be evaluated often within your organization to gauge your progress. Once lag measures are set, it's time to create lead measures and a monthly scorecard to make sure that you reach your WIG.

3. A big differentiator in churches is if the ministry is gifts based or needs based.

   » **CHALLENGE:** Take a look at your discipleship track to see if you can identify whether it is a method of helping people find their gifts and putting those gifts to work toward their purpose. Many discipleship tracks are based on only spiritual enrichment, which they should be, but they should also be the first step in people understanding how they can make a difference by serving in the local church.

4. 10-3-1: The goals that set the course.

   » **CHALLENGE:** Take a moment to assess where you want to be in ten years' time. This is likely the start of determining what you need to do in the three-year term as well as the one-year term to accomplish those goals.

HOW TO ESTABLISH THE BUDGET FRAMEWORK AND TRAIN THE STAFF

"Used correctly, a budget doesn't restrict
you; it empowers you." —TERE STOUFFER

"A budget is not just a collection of numbers, but an
expression of our values and aspirations." —JACK LEW

"I hated every minute of training, but I said,
'Don't quit. Suffer now and live the rest of your
life as a champion.'" —MUHAMMAD ALI

"Tell me and I forget, teach me and I may remember,
involve me and I learn." —BENJAMIN FRANKLIN

When Tracy and I initially prepared to launch Grow Church, we sought wisdom and guidance from those who had previously forged the same path we were about to embark upon. Two organizations whose experience and input most significantly impacted us were The Association of Related Churches (ARCChurches.com) and Church of the Highlands (ChurchoftheHighlands.com). Their resources gave us starting points, simple processes, and a healthy outlook on ministry, many of which are incorporated into the material presented in this book.

Tracy and I wanted the framework for our first budget to be simple; now, however, after years of astounding growth, we still maintain the basic four-category-budget framework that has served us so well. Here it is:

- Giving 10%
- Savings 10%
- Employees and services 35%
- Ministry operations and building 45%

On pages 160–161 is a current Grow Church sample budget that shows the breakdown of expense categories. To see a color-coded version of this budget, go to GrowMyChurch.com

Operating within the framework of a budget isn't easy at first, because most of the time a church's needs are greater than its finances. It takes self-control and dedication to operate successfully within a budget, which is why I recommend that nobody do it alone. At Grow Church we've established an executive oversight committee to hold us accountable.

As described in chapter 5, our board of trustees serves as our fiduciary responsibility team. We do not pay our board members for their service, though they have extensive business backgrounds with large organizations, entrepreneurial organizations, and churches. Having people with this kind of experience is crucial to the success of the church.

I have confidence that our trustees will always make decisions in the best interest of the church—especially when a project requires a supernatural dose of faith to see it come to fruition.

Now let's examine each of the four categories of the budget.

GIVING

Remember this: Whoever sows sparingly will also reap sparingly, and whoever sows generously will also reap generously. Each of you should give what you have decided in your heart to give, not reluctantly or under compulsion, for God loves a cheerful giver. And God is able to bless you abundantly, so that in all things and at all times, having all that you need, you will abound in every good work (2 CORINTHIANS 9:6–8 NIV).

Giving is my favorite category of the budget because it is what makes the Church the hope of the world. For the local church, giving is the way we tell the community we are here, we love them, and they don't have to do anything to earn our love and care. Giving is the most crucial part of the budget.

(*continued on page 161*)

SAMPLE BUDGET

	CURRENT YEAR	%
INCOME		
4005 - Donations - General		
4010 - Donations - Legacy		
4015 - Donations - Missions Trips		
4020 - Donations - Students		
4025 - Donations - Kids		
4110 - Tuition - Grow School of Ministry		
4115 - Event Registrations		
4120 - Grow Store		
4125 - Interest Income		
4140 - Rebates Income		
4205 - Lease / Rentals		
SUBTOTAL INCOME		
OPERATING EXPENSES		
6005 Accounting		
6010 Admin - Office & Supplies		
6015 Admin - Dues & Subscriptions		
6020 Benefits		
6025 Executive		
6030 Facilities - Maintenance		
6035 Facilities - Supplies		
6040 Facilities - Utilities		
6045 Facilities - Insurance		
6050 Human Resources		
6055 IT		
6060 Legal		
6065 Marketing		
6070 Payroll		
6075 Payroll - WC Insurance		
6080 Payroll - Payroll Taxes		
6085 Payroll - Subscription		
6090 Recruiting & Onboarding		
SUBTOTAL OPERATING EXPENSES		
MINISTRY EXPENSES		
7005 Baptism		
7010 Creative		
7015 Events (Registered)		
7016 Events		
7020 Grow Groups		
7025 Grow Kids		
7030 Grow Steps		
7035 Grow Store		
7040 Grow Students		
7045 Grow Teams		
7050 Grow Worship		
7051 Grow Young Adults		
7055 Hispanic		
7060 Legacy		
7065 Missions		
7070 Missions Trips		
7075 Outreach		
7080 Grow Care		
7085 Production		
7305 GSM		
SUBTOTAL MINISTRY EXPENSES		
Savings		
SUBTOTAL SAVINGS		
NET INCOME		

	ACTUAL TOTAL		ACTUAL %		GOAL %		GOAL AMOUNTS
Missions					10%		
Employees/Services					35%		
Ministry Ops/Bldg					45%		
Savings					10%		
GRAND TOTAL EXPENSES					100%		

(*continued from page 159*)

Growing a healthy church requires establishing margin in all line items—and giving is no exception. By releasing 90 percent of the amount budgeted for giving each month (based on the previous year's total income), we always have the funds to help should there be an event such as a catastrophic disaster in our state or the nation.

Operating in this fashion brings up the logical question, What happens when the church's income in the present year is far

There is no pressure in this series to give; it's just an opportunity to close out the year with praise for what God has done and, by faith, what He is going to do in the year ahead.

greater than the budgeted amount projected at 90 percent of the previous year's income? This has always been the case at Grow Church; therefore, we make up the difference twice each year, in June and December, since our fiscal year ends in June and the end of calendar year falls near Christmas.

Our missions director starts by assembling a list of needs from the organizations we currently support, as well as any other outside ministry needs brought to our attention. We discuss with the board of trustees the amount of excess funds designated for giving, after which we assign percentages of the overage to each of the chosen organizations. There is nothing more fun or rewarding than the process of writing big checks that will make such a positive impact in the lives of people. And I confess that doing so has turned me into a hardcore "giving addict."

A concept that we've implemented over the past few years is our Legacy Offering, a term we got from Church of the Highlands. The Legacy Offering is a very special annual moment for Grow Church that engages the congregation in a one-time, over-and-above gift to close out the year. It's usually the last message in a series dedicated to giving, generosity, or stewardship, and that final message is usually delivered about three weeks prior to the end of the year. We talk about the Legacy Offering for a month leading into Legacy Sunday (the over-and-above gift collection Sunday), because we don't want it to be a surprise to the congregation. We want people to seek the heart of God for how He would ask them to participate.

There is no pressure in this series to give; it's just an opportunity to close out the year with praise for what God has done and, by faith, what He is going to do in the year ahead. Since we started this end-of-year offering, it has doubled our giving outside of the church to local, national, and international missions. This is what takes our 10 percent-budgeted giving to levels of 20–25 percent annually. There is such an energy that is built around this annual moment, and it is such a blessing to the church and community.

SAVINGS

The plans of the diligent lead to profit as surely as
haste leads to poverty **(PROVERBS 21:5 NIV).**

We've learned that it's impossible for the church to grow without a planned savings approach that enables us to respond when God says *go!* For instance, when God opens the door for a new building, we will be ready to move forward. Our commitment to living in a constant state of saving enables us to always be on track with God's plans and purposes for Grow Church. This is how He works.

Since our savings account is not to be touched, we've set up a 501(c) (2) holding company, into which we "sweep" anything over our necessary monthly operating funds plus $100,000. Our savings account holds a safety net of $100,000.

Our checking account is for operations and cash flow, and the holding company holds the rest, including all assets valued at over $2,500. This setup is the safest way we've found to separate the church operating account from our excess funds account and reserve account. It provides a nice safety wall against any litigation that may come against the church in that the operating account is the only one in jeopardy of litigation. The holdings company has a separate board of trustees, so it is actually a completely separate entity to keep it safe.

More detailed information about our holding company, as well as information about our endowment fund, is included in the Addendum at the back of the book.

EMPLOYEES AND SERVICES

Whatever you do, work at it with all your heart, as working for the Lord, not for human masters (COLOSSIANS 3:23 NIV).

This category of the budget consists of any items that support the employees of the church, including benefits, health coverage, 401k plan matching, and employment taxes, to name a few.

As with any church or business, an organization is only as good as the staff members it can keep; therefore, a benefit package should always grow and improve. When it comes to letting our staff know how much we appreciate them, a great benefit package speaks louder than actual words.

You may ask, "Pastor James, how do I go about putting together a great benefit package for my church staff?" Tracy and I wondered the same thing when we sat down to put together our first package. We wanted to be competitive with other employers in our area, so we did some research and found the company that earned the title of "best place to work in the city" and modeled our benefit package after theirs.

Of course, at that time we didn't have near the assets they had to work with; however, what we did have was faith and determination to start small and grow our benefit package every year. I recall how wonderful it felt the first time our package grew by $60,000 in one year—and then repeated that growth again the next year. I've learned that any church who wants the best staff needs to treat them as such.

Sadly, throughout my Christian life I've witnessed what I describe as abusive church leadership. I've known of staff members who have served the church for twenty, thirty, or forty years and have nothing to show for it at the end of their careers. This isn't right and shouldn't be acceptable.

At Grow Church, we endeavor to find ways to demonstrate our love for our staff members more each year, and the way we do it is through our benefit package. A copy of our benefit package is included in the Addendum of this book.

MINISTRY OPERATIONS AND BUILDING

So the Twelve gathered all the disciples together and said, "It would not be right for us to neglect the ministry of the word of God in order to wait on tables. Brothers and sisters, choose seven men from among you who are known to be full of the Spirit and wisdom. We will turn this responsibility over to them and will give our attention to prayer and the ministry of the word" (ACTS 6:2–4 NIV).

This area of the budget includes two components. *Ministry operations* entails any in-church programs and activities such as our student ministry, children's ministry, hospitality, administration, serving teams, and small groups, to name a few. The *building* component comprises any expense directly impacting the building. These expenses include capital expenditures such as air conditioning units, printers, paving, tree trimming, supplies, painting, flooring, installations, and servicing the building. Of course, building expenses also include insurance and would additionally include a mortgage (if we had one).

Though at one time we included *capital expenditures* in the annual budget, we now designate them separately as *capital investments*, depreciated over time and held on the balance sheet instead of the income statement (accountant jargon). We've set capital investments as anything over $2,500 in value.

PREPARING OUR ANNUAL BUDGET

"Suppose one of you wants to build a tower. Won't you first sit down and estimate the cost to see if you have enough money to complete it?" (LUKE 14:27 NIV).

Immediately after we celebrate Easter, our staff and teams begin plans for our upcoming budgets and fiscal year calendar that begins July 1. As such, our first budget review for the next fiscal year occurs the first or second week of May. We then have a couple of weeks to work with our teams to crunch their numbers before submitting them to the board of trustees for approval around the end of May. We have a specific process for this preparation because it needs to stay within the agreed upon 90 percent of the previous year's income. I meet with the accountant and staff director prior to rolling these numbers out so that we can break down each department's goal amounts. This process helps the directors in their pursuit of budgeting for the following year.

We then have a month to make any modifications or changes we may need to direct to the trustees prior to the last board meeting of the fiscal year, held at the end of June. In this way, we have an approved budget and annual calendar to move forward with in the new fiscal year.

As long as we keep our priorities in focus, our calendar and budget will remain in sync. In October we again review the entire calendar and budget with the directors in case we need to request any changes to the board for the November trustee meeting or the last meeting of the calendar year in December. This process generally works quite well because it allows us to keep the trustees informed on how we're aligning with the budget and of any challenges we've encountered along the way. We also evaluate our income goals to see how close we are to our budgeted goals so that the trustees feel comfortable throughout the process.

ESTABLISHING LINE-ITEM MANAGERS

That the man of God may be complete, thoroughly equipped for every good work (2 TIMOTHY 3:17).

Before giving our directors a line item to manage in the budget, we take them through a training process to help ensure their success. We like to be assured that each of our directors has a good grip on his or her personal finances, because good money management begins at home. Those who can't manage their personal budgets certainly can't manage a budget on the job or at the church. Directors at Grow Church oversee their line items on the budget, so good money-management skills are imperative for their success in that role. However, not everyone comes from the same background or upbringing, so we train them in the role of director prior to their getting a line item to manage.

My wife and I want to be sure line-item managers (or "directors") are generous with their time and resources. This practice is helpful so that they understand the weight of responsibility that comes with managing their church-budget line. Each of our directors manages his or her area of the budget. Directors are overseen by the staff director, who is overseen by the executive pastor. The executive pastor is overseen by the board of trustees. Checks, balances, and accountability are crucial to the health of the church.

> *A healthy church with checks, balances, and accountability will keep you in ministry for years to come ...*

When it comes to staff members, we can't force them to run their lives by way of a personal budget, but we can most certainly talk about it frequently and present the practice as the best way to win in life. Staff members who successfully live within their personal budgets don't have to ask for an early release of their payroll checks so that they can pay their bills.

Now let me speak directly to you: A healthy church with checks, balances, and accountability will keep you in ministry for years to come, but a financially unhealthy church will get you out of ministry early because it isn't set up correctly. Accountable teams win in the long run—and we all want to win.

STANDARD OPERATING PROCEDURES (SOPS)

Then He said to them, "Follow Me, and I will make you fishers of men" (MATTHEW 4:19).

Clear and concise standard operating procedures (SOPs) are crucial for the success of the church, and for training others to lead in ministry. A written directory of SOPs ensures that processes and procedures are duplicatable across the entire church.

We challenge our SOPs frequently to keep them relevant, and during planning meetings we often ask, "Is there an SOP for this situation?" Our directors review SOPs monthly and modify them if needed to ensure we always have up-to-date training materials for new volunteers or staff members. Some of our SOPs are demonstrated in video form so that we can show, rather than tell, how things are done. This process makes our systems repeatable, and repeatability is necessary when you have so many volunteers and staff serving in so many areas of ministry.

Every process and procedure, especially those conducted during weekly services, should have an SOP attached to it to ensure it's done the same way regardless of who is serving at any given service. Grow Church has a multitude of volunteers, and having SOPs in place is our way of ensuring excellence in all areas.

We consider our SOPs the "secret sauce" that results in many positive comments from people such as, "Wow—your church does everything with excellence!"

REQUISITIONS

The soul of a lazy man desires, and has nothing; but the soul of the diligent shall be made rich (**PROVERBS 13:4**).

Having a system for handling requisitions is the best way to stay on financial track within the safety of accountability.

Requisitions are the vehicles through which church money is spent. The process goes like this: When a member of the staff needs to spend money, he or she fills out a requisition form and submits it to his or her director. The director then checks the budget and either challenges the requisition or approves it, since the director is familiar with the numbers in that area of ministry and knows how the budget is tracking financially. Once the director signs off on the requisition, the item can be ordered or put on the ministry credit card. The requisition is then filed so that everyone knows who approved it, and the process can be tracked all the way to purchase. After the purchase the receipt is attached to the order and filed for future reference if needed.

Though checks may be requested, only a few signers are on the church account—me and my wife, plus two board members for when Tracy and I are out of town. Though Tracy and I are supposed to sign all checks because we oversee day-to-day operations of the church, we've trained our directors to such a level that we trust them to run the system appropriately. We've built enough checks and balances into our system that we are comfortable with directors spending out of their budgets so long as they don't go over. Nobody goes over the approved budget without special approval beforehand. This policy is well known to our staff.

DIRECTOR DATA ACCESS FOR FUTURE SUCCESS

> *"Go therefore and make disciples of all the nations,*
> *baptizing them in the name of the Father and of the Son*
> *and of the Holy Spirit, teaching them to observe all things*
> *that I have commanded you; and lo, I am with you always,*
> *even to the end of the age"* (MATTHEW 28:19–20).

Once we have put together processes for accountability and trained directors to own the budget, the next step is to ensure they have access to data. We accomplish this gain of access through monthly meetings in which each director meets with either the staff director or someone from the administrative team to see how they did the previous month and where they stand for the remainder of the year.

Church budgets have what I refer to as hot seasons and cold seasons of spending. For instance, February and March are usually busy (hot) spending months because that's when we need to make all our purchases for Easter. Directors are aware of this time of increased spending and work with the accounting department to setup premeditated spikes in their budgets.

We are better able to equip ourselves for a budget versus actual comparison by adjusting our accounting software to accept higher spending months in the calculation. We typically divide budgets by the number twelve to establish an average monthly income/

expense figure; however, for better control and understanding for monthly reporting, we can anticipate the higher-spending months and calculate them into the budget versus actual numbers.

Our directors have access at all times to the accounting department, who sends out monthly reports to all directors. Our bookkeeper is available to discuss any issues and is trained to help the directors with budgets, keep them accountable, and get the appropriate approval and signatures for spending. We've created a great team environment that we certainly appreciate.

STAFF BUDGET CONTROLS

The wise have wealth and luxury, but fools spend whatever they get (PROVERBS 21:20 NLT).

When we first implemented budget controls, Grow Church was much smaller than it is today. In the early years we had two or three people responsible for the budget; at the time of this writing, we have fifteen responsible for the budget in their areas of ministry. Of course, some directors oversee multiple areas of the budget because they oversee more than one area of ministry.

The budget needs to be controlled by a director who holds budgetary line items in the utmost respect and understands that the success or failure to perform the job directly affects his or her job. This statement is not intended to convey a threat; rather, it enforces our commitment to the highest accountability for the budget to be owned by our directors.

All areas of ministry fall under or within a director's oversight from a budget perspective. The responsibility for every dollar spent lies with a director, and that director is accountable to the staff director, who is accountable to the executive pastor. This process ensures the church's finances are governed by accountability.

Every process has an accountability system tied to it to ensure everyone's safety against questions that could put an individual at the risk of scrutiny.

When a volunteer has an expense or needs to purchase something for an area of ministry, he or she fills out a requisition form and submits it to the director of that area for approval and a signature. Then the staff director signs the form (if in agreement with it) and sends it to bookkeeping to be processed. Every process has an accountability system tied to it to ensure everyone's safety against questions that could put an individual at the risk of scrutiny.

If the processes are accountable, everything and everyone is safe, which allows all staff members to flow in their gifts and not have to question if they should or shouldn't have something approved. At Grow Church, our directors feel free to make decisions necessary for growth and forward progress without wondering if they might get in trouble. It's freeing to have the ability to work like this.

MEETINGS AND COMMUNICATIONS

And above all things have fervent love for one another,
for "love will cover a multitude of sins." Be hospitable to
one another without grumbling. As each one has received
a gift, minister it to one another, as good stewards
of the manifold grace of God (1 PETER 4:8–10).

Effective communication is critical to any organizational system and, for us, to keep our directors moving forward. For this reason our staff director meets with each director once each week for a minimum of fifteen minutes and a maximum of thirty minutes. These meetings focus on weekly objectives and any issues that may get in the director's way of accomplishing those objectives.

We encourage directors not to attempt to accomplish objectives alone but to allow volunteers to help. In so doing, directors help keep everyone on the same page as they build their volunteer teams. Our staff director encourages and challenges the directors to build teams, because this is the life blood of a growing church.

Our weekly directors' meeting is a time when we first pray and worship together before we follow up on any agenda items created at the individual meetings with the staff director. Worshiping and praying is crucial because this is not just a business but a team of people called by God to hear from Him and build the church. Creating an agenda with notes, responsibilities, and deadlines is also crucial. We never leave a directors' meeting without establishing responsibilities and deadlines for each action item. We've found that taking the time to put all decisions into writing is the only way to keep us pushing the church forward. This is also the meeting where all the directors get the necessary input for their upcoming weekly meetings with their departments.

We take care to ensure information doesn't pass through the departments or volunteer teams until it is approved to do so. Therefore, we make sure to follow the protocol of communications in this order: overseers (if necessary), trustees, pastors, directors, entire staff, Grow Team leaders, Grow Group leaders, then the congregation. We make sure in the weekly directors' meeting to identify anything the directors are expected to communicate from the meeting to their teams. This helps us communicate clearly and effectively to the entire church.

We think excellence happens on purpose, so recognizing and addressing opportunities continues to make us better the following week.

We can also take the time to frame out the way we are going to communicate a specific topic so that we all communicate it the same way. Oftentimes we practice the communication on each other so that the directors are aware of how the topic is going to be communicated to the rest of the church. This keeps us all in sync and avoids future questions that may arise.

We have a weekly production meeting to review the previous weekend services and plan for the upcoming weekend services. We adhere to a standard in this meeting, and many of our other meetings, that we call "wins and opportunities." *Wins* are the things that went well in the previous weekend service. *Opportunities* are the things that could use some adjustments to make them better.

We always start with the wins so that everyone feels encouraged. During the portion of the meeting where we celebrate the wins, it's not unusual to hear this rowdy bunch of people start an in-unison slow clap for someone who did something out of the ordinary and amazing. The slow clap builds speed and energy as it continues until the room is filled with loud, fast clapping. This special recognition happens when an individual has gone out of his or her way for someone else or has done something super special. There are always a lot of wins, and we don't want to avoid giving credit for them. There are also always opportunities to discuss. We think excellence happens on purpose, so recognizing and addressing opportunities continues to make us better the following week.

In this weekly production meeting, we review the Planning Center (an electronic organizational system for churches) order of service for the upcoming week and decide how it is going to function, as well as who is going to oversee each section of it. This review helps us prepare all the directors for their weekend roles and notify them of any changes to the order of service.

We create an order of service for every event at the church, because order of service helps us streamline the event from start to finish and communicate all the necessary roles required to make it excellent.

After this meeting, we have a straightforward plan for the upcoming weekend, which gives us a straightforward plan in preparation for the work week.

CHAPTER NINE REVIEW:

1. A simple four-category budget will help you evaluate your organization.

   » **CHALLENGE:** Break down your organization's budget into four categories for simple and consistent evaluation. Remember, the four categories are giving, savings, employees and services, and ministry operations and building.

2. An organization's giving dictates the outpouring of blessing it will experience.

   » **CHALLENGE:** Evaluate different organizations in your area that fit well into your vision of reaching your city with the gospel. Maybe start with the poor, widow, orphan, and prisoner (according to the Bible) as avenues to give to in your community.

3. You are ready to do what God says to do, when He says to do it.

   » **CHALLENGE:** Your savings will come in handy in the future when God starts to speak to you about His agenda for the community that you serve. Communicate to your staff how we are to do our part and God does His.

4. For my whole life, I've seen pastors retire with nothing. This goes for church staff as well.

   » **CHALLENGE:** Take a step toward training and offering some tools to your staff that will help them prepare for the future.

_____

_____

_____

_____

_____

_____

TRUE STORY: RED TO BLACK IN ONE YEAR—FINDING MARGIN FOR GROWTH

"A life lived without borders is a life lived in captivity."
—TODD STOCKER

"You must create more margin so you have room for what's important, not merely urgent." —MICHAEL HYATT

"Money is a terrible master but an excellent servant."
—P. T. BARNUM

"If I had to run a company on three measures, those measures would be customer satisfaction, employee satisfaction, and cash flow." —JACK WELCH

While on Grow Church mission trips to South America, I connected with a church that had successfully grown into a megachurch with an attendance of about eight thousand people. They'd also established so many foundations and organizations outside the church that their city had been greatly impacted by their work.

When I was in the area I often spent time at the church to learn how they did the things that caused them to be so successful. Of course, South-American culture is markedly different than North-American culture, but there were still plenty of concepts and procedures that would benefit Tracy and me as we guided the growth of our church in Naples.

You can imagine my surprise when leaders of the South American church asked for my help. Why would the leadership of an established and successful megachurch need *my* input? I quickly understood *exactly* why they needed help when I saw their profit and loss statement, balance sheet, and budget information, which they'd supplied for my review prior to my first visit with their leadership.

I discovered that instead of pulling ahead financially each year, the church remained at a consistent net zero, meaning it had neither a financial surplus nor a financial deficit. They had operated in that manner for the preceding thirty to forty years. At the time they asked for my help, they desperately needed a new facility for their church, but they had absolutely no money in savings to accomplish that task. As we all know, it takes money to purchase or build a large facility—or any facility at all.

Since none of the leaders of that great church had a business or financial background, my first task was to familiarize them with some basic financial concepts and stats based on my personal experience. I started with some quick math.

Let's say an established church is interested in purchasing a facility priced fairly at $5 million. To get any bank interested in making a loan, the church should expect to make a down payment of $2 million. Churches are historically not recognized by banks as financially trustworthy organizations, and rightly so, because most church leaders lack both training and experience in business and banking. This makes churches a risky investment.

As a seasoned and successful investor in both commercial and residential real estate, I always recommend giving a bank or lending institution *more* than the required minimum down payment. I've found that being at better than 50 percent loan-to-value (LTV) ratio on a property is a good place to be, even in a down economy. (Remember, loan-to-value ratio is the figure that lenders use to determine how much risk they have on a secured loan, which measures the relationship between the loan amount and the market value of the property.)

So, for our hypothetical church that is interested in purchasing that $5 million facility, I'd recommend they first save $2.5 million to use as a minimum down payment. Another safe choice for consideration is to lease the property with an option to purchase, which allows the church to operate without debt until it has a safe margin in the property. This is the kind of margin I define as having the money it takes to do what God says to do, when He says to do it.

After going over these scenarios with the leadership of the South American church, they understood the direction I was about to take them. They didn't have a big down payment saved up, but they needed one desperately. They were on board with the process as we took the necessary steps together toward creating a healthy church.

STEP ONE: COLLECT DATA

"And to one he gave five talents, to another two, and to another one, to each according to his own ability; and immediately he went on a journey" (MATTHEW 25:15).

I started by asking for the past three years' annual income statements, a year-to-date income statement, balance sheets from the past three years, a breakdown of salaries and job titles, as well as any available budgetary information. Once I had these reports in hand, my job was to go to work on the numbers so that I could make some assessments in preparation for our meeting. Their job was to be prepared to answer the following set of questions I left with them:

1. What do you feel are the church's top five priorities?

2. Are you happy with the return-on-investment (ROI) you experience at your weekend services? The ROI entails the number of salvations, rededications

to Jesus, baptisms, and other significant steps
forward in one's walk with the Lord.

3. Are you happy with the number of people who volunteer
   to serve at weekend services and other events?

4. Do you feel you have enough money to do what
   God says to do, when He says to do it?

5. Do you have in place a clear process of approval to
   get the funds needed for all the church's initiatives?

I was confident I'd know the answers to these questions by
the time I finished assessing their numbers, but I wanted to see
how their answers stacked up to how I thought they'd answer
after the numbers review. But numbers don't lie, so following the
money is always the best way to identify a church's priorities.

Working with the breakdown of salaries and job titles, I started
with the five key roles in the church and then added two more to
make the total number of seven categories:

- worship
- administration
- technical/production
- students
- children
- pastoral care
- volunteer teams

I assigned a color to each category, and then took each staff position and placed it in one of those seven color-coded categories so that I could determine how much money was being spent in each area. Doing this would help determine where their actual focus was, even if they thought otherwise (because numbers don't lie).

I've found this exercise a valuable tool for churches who want to better understand where they're spending their money. The results are oftentimes surprising to organizations when they find that, over time, they've veered away from their core objectives. It's always gratifying to audit churches in this way and see them discover facts helpful in getting them back on focus for maximum kingdom impact.

I continued to work with the financial numbers the leaders of the South American church had given me to determine their overall growth from year to year. The easiest way to get the information was to simply look at the bottom-line income from donations only, which oftentimes is a fair representation of growth in attendance numbers as well. The exception is large givers who are not regular givers in a particular year. I knew that by reading the church's income numbers, which can be easily measured, I'd be able to get a handle on its growth rate.

I like to see a church grow, year over year, at a rate of about 10–20 percent. Ten percent growth is a really good number while 20 percent can be hard to keep up with, though it's a good problem to have. If a church is growing, then we can assess how to find some margin in its operating funds.

I wasn't yet sure of the growth rate of the South American church, but I would find out as I continued the financial diagnostic process.

STEP TWO: COLOR-CODED BREAKDOWN

"Write the vision and make it plain on tablets" (HABAKKUK 2:2).

I took the church's entire income statement and broke it into categories as I'd done with the salaries and income from donations only, and then I color-coded every category. Obviously, this megachurch had considerably more categories than a small church would, which meant I had to be a bit more creative with my colors, but I got the job done.

I've learned that by color-coding categories, the numbers are easier to grasp in the context of the church's priorities. Colors quickly identify the area of greatest spending, which is always indicative of the church's highest priority. The second largest area of spending represents the church's second highest priority. It's not uncommon to see church leadership express surprise when they see the reality of their numbers. Some may dispute the correlation between numbers and priorities, but in the end they realize this exercise is for their benefit. The results are not wrong; rather, they reflect current priorities. Priorities can always change, but they won't unless the facts are reviewed and new policies and strategies are set in place.

Armed with enough information to start some discussions, I was ready for our first meeting. As expected, the group was astonished at my assessment of their priorities, but after evaluating those priorities they agreed to make some changes. Although they could make simpler changes immediately, they would need to make others over the course of several months.

Oftentimes, the most significant changes are effective only when decisions are thought through and implemented with precision. Too many big changes implemented too frequently can result in loss of motivation for the church staff and volunteers.

With the color codes broken down and changes ready to implement, I turned my focus to the church budget. Theirs had been set in place at the beginning of the year, so my strategy was to help them establish basic parameters for the following year's budget. The first parameter was that the proposed budget would be 90 percent of the present year's budget. I then broke the budget into the four areas and percentages discussed in chapter 9:

- Giving..10%
- Savings 10%
- Employees and services 35%
- Ministry operations and building................45%

I wasn't overly concerned with the percentage breakdown. I wanted to get their previous year's numbers plugged into these four categories so that we could challenge the numbers and then reshape them in line with the principle of marginal budgeting. It turned out their current numbers were far off the target percentages, but knowing the facts is half the battle in becoming financially healthy.

A church that doesn't first know where its money is going can't make a course correction. As the saying goes, Knowledge is power. But I've learned that budgeting is also power.

STEP THREE: A CRITICAL REVIEW

"But you, be strong and do not let your hands be weak, for your work shall be rewarded! (2 CHRONICLES 15:7).

When we reviewed the newly color-coded *employees and services* area of the budget, it was apparent to all that there were a lot of "pastor" titles on the salaries sheet, which put pastoral care at the top of the list of expenses.

I figured that was a good time to announce to the leadership that at Grow Church we don't pay our pastors to pastor. The minute I said those words, I heard a collective *gasp* from those in attendance. I thought, *This is it—I'll be thrown out of the country for good.* But they didn't throw me out; instead, they asked me to explain that statement, so I told them how Grow Church pays people to build teams, not pastor people. Sure, building teams involves pastoring people, but building teams is key to growing a healthy church. We pay our pastoral care pastor at Grow Church to build a volunteer team of other people who are called to pastor, so that we can use their God-given gifts in ministry to fulfill their purpose in life.

I allowed them a few moments to process what I'd just told them, and then talked to them about the importance of hiring people to build teams instead of doing tasks, people who will lead others into volunteer leadership roles instead of creating a culture of hirelings. They continued to listen and ponder, so I continued to press forward in identifying areas where they required change to bring the church to optimal health, and then I suggested what those changes should be.

Later, when I met privately with the lead pastors and executive team only, I turned their attention to the church's board of trustees, all of whom were pastors. Churches require spiritual oversight, and this church had plenty of it; however, trustees also have a fiduciary responsibility to the church. The problem with that group of trustees was that they were not business savvy; not one trustee had owned a business or earned a business degree. They were all pastors who may or may not have graduated from seminary only.

I suggested we take a fresh look at the trustees and separate them into two groups: one would provide spiritual oversight and the other would have fiduciary responsibility. We accomplished the task by asking each trustee this question: If you could serve on only one of these groups, which are you best suited for? This was a complicated question for most of them, so we gave them a couple of days to consider their answers.

As I'd expected, most felt they could best be of service on the spiritual oversight group. Though several of these leaders had a small amount of experience in accounting, there were other members of the church who had strong backgrounds and experience in that field as well as in finances, business, and law. The change didn't happen overnight, but eventually current members of the board were steered toward serving in areas that matched their gifts and callings, while other individuals were invited to join the board on the basis of their business experience. We eventually had two groups we called the Spiritual Advisory Group and the Board of Trustees.

We had much to cover, more than time would allow in that initial meeting. Over the next twelve months, I returned to South America three more times to meet with the leaders and help them assess their situation, measure their results, and evaluate their spiritual ROI (return on investment). Remember, in the church world ROI doesn't mean money; rather, it has to do with impact. Impact can mean the number of souls saved, the number of those delivered from drugs and alcohol, the number of marriages restored, and the list goes on.

STEP FOUR: CHURCH FOCUS

Let your eyes look straight ahead, and your eyelids
look right before you (PROVERBS 4:25).

Each church has its own God-given vision and calling, and to successfully fulfill that calling, every program, activity, and outreach should be measured with this one question: Does it line up with the vision and calling of the church? We found the South American church had invested money in many good ideas; however, not all were God-given ideas. The result was no measurable ROI, only a drain on the budget.

Some of the programs the church started in recent years had never been assessed from the beginning. In other words, leadership had never evaluated the programs in a strategic budget with an ROI assessment prior to their being launched. What I mean by a *strategic budget* is a financial proposal for the programs prior to launch.

Reviewing and approving strategic budgets and evaluating ROIs before launch enables a board of trustees to understand the program and evaluate it appropriately. In the case of this South American church, the collective drain on the budget proved a major factor in preventing the church from being in the black, which would have put it in a positive financial position on an annual basis.

While the matter was certainly not easy to discuss, we got through it and made some difficult changes that helped steer the church toward financial health.

Another change of direction took place with the staffing as we looked for effective ways to transition staff members to areas that better fit their individual gifts and callings. For example, the church was paying some individuals solely to pastor a specific area of the church. While pastoring is a noble role and calling, I suggested expanding the individuals' effectiveness by creating detailed job descriptions that set specific goals to be met throughout the year, which involved building volunteer teams as well as establishing a set schedule of office hours and an accountable reporting system through the board of trustees.

All staff members need to report to someone who will hold them accountable in their roles. As we put staff positions under the spotlight throughout the year, we discovered some weak areas. The goal was then to transition individuals into new roles;

however, the few who couldn't make the change were transitioned out of their positions.

Each staff position requires an individual who understands and is committed to the church's focus and goals. A church staff working together to accomplish set goals impacts finances in a positive way and produces a healthy church.

STEP FIVE: SPOTLIGHT TOP PRIORITIES

For those who live according to the flesh set their minds on the things of the flesh, but those who live according to the Spirit, the things of the Spirit (ROMANS 8:5).

The more the church leaders and I worked together through the budget, the clearer priorities became as we cut, moved, and modified the vision relating to church initiatives.

In chapter 5 I shared Grow Church's four priorities in ministry, which serve as the foundation for every budget we make. If a proposed initiative doesn't fit within these four priorities, we don't do it.

After I talked with the South American church leadership, we determined the top four priorities for their church, which I color-coded so that we could better understand the church's needs pertaining to growth and health. We discovered the church was growing in members, but their volunteer teams were not simultaneously growing. A closer examination revealed the cause of the lack of growth in the teams: the church had under-funded their volunteer recruiting process and had done little marketing. They were getting the results of what the numbers showed us.

The church needed to place an emphasis on volunteerism, so I set the priorities for change on the basis of our success in building volunteer teams at Grow Church. I began by describing the process we use, and the value we found, through incorporating the *DiSC®* personality profile and *StrengthsFinder* assessment in helping people understand their purpose and calling (see chapter 8). I shared that once people see themselves as the unique individuals God created them to be, they can easily gravitate to the area of service within the church where their giftings can be best utilized and where they will be most fulfilled.

Next, leadership needed to find ways to honor in a more meaningful and significant way those members currently serving at the church. The volunteers needed something to be excited about. I explained the value in using money and resources intentionally to grow their teams, and the fact that when the payoff came a little further down the road, the investment would be well worth it.

Churches oftentimes fail to remember that volunteers are virtually free labor—but they should never be treated as such. Volunteers should always be treated with the highest respect and honor. To serve as inspiration for their own initiative, I told the leaders about some of the things we did at Grow Church to honor our volunteers.

For example, during services and events we have a special area reserved for volunteers where they can get snacks and beverages. Along the walls are lockers to ensure their belongings are secure while they serve in their designated areas. Volunteers also receive discounts at our church store, where they will find books, clothing, and our special brand of promotional items. And several times each year we sponsor special events to honor our volunteers. We like to bless the people God sends to help us and honor the gifts He has placed in each of them. After all, if none of them showed up on the weekend, we couldn't reach our goal of seeing people come to Jesus. I concluded the discussion about volunteers with this fact: the more we honor our volunteers at Grow Church, the more enthusiastic they are about recruiting others to join them.

Just as I'd done with the area of volunteerism, I addressed each of the church's top priorities and created an initial growth strategy for each one.

STEP SIX: EVALUATE, ENCOURAGE, CHALLENGE

*"For I, the LORD your God, will hold your right hand,
saying to you, 'Fear not, I will help you'"* (ISAIAH 41:13).

After I'd made all my recommendations and received the buy-in from church leaders, we agreed I'd come back to evaluate progress in a few months. However, when I returned as scheduled, I learned they'd hired two new people without first transitioning existing staff members to their new locations. I was surprised to learn this, but not upset. After all, they'd requested my services as a consultant, not a church leader.

I shared with them my concern that our consulting arrangement might be a waste of both my time and theirs since they were unwilling to move according to instruction to find margin in their finances. I delivered the comment in such a kind and honoring manner that none of the leaders took offense. They agreed they'd made decisions outside the safety parameters we'd established and would take the necessary steps to tighten up the new processes and procedures.

I was working with a group of church leaders who really wanted to make good changes but didn't yet have the muscle to do so. I needed to make some changes in strategy, so I put together some simpler guides for them to implement over the next few months. The good news was, I wouldn't have to take a trip to South America for the follow-up evaluation; it could be done via a Zoom call. And now for the *really* good news: In less than one year, I joined them for a celebratory assessment of their finances and business moves. They were in the black (a positive financial situation) for the first time in forty years!

I was so proud of them.

The church in South America adopted many of the procedures that have helped Grow Church become the healthy church it is today. And I'm happy to tell you that since doing so, that church has gained margin in its finances, undergone growth in all areas, and experienced success and health as never before.

CHAPTER TEN REVIEW:

1. A plan to go from red to black is essential.
   » **CHALLENGE:** Prepare your church for continual growth by setting up a system of saving for future building projects and a larger building.

2. 50 percent loan-to-value ratio is recommended.
   » **CHALLENGE:** Since you've already started thinking about your ten-year plan, consider dreaming about the size of facility necessary to accommodate your vision for growth, and then put a plan together to save half of the required amount starting now.

3. Data collection is important to understand your organization.
   » **CHALLENGE:** Collect the data that will help you see what your current priorities are according to the numbers. If numbers don't lie, and they don't, then doing this is crucial to get your priorities on track.

4. Paying staff to build teams, not just to do work, is vital to healthy church growth.
   » **CHALLENGE:** Having your staff devote time to team building is usually a hard pill to swallow, I know, and it starts with a whole lot of coaching. Start to discuss this concept with your staff; it's never too early to start the conversation.

_____

_____

_____

_____

_____

_____

_____

HOW TO TRIAGE YOUR CHURCH

"We were front line trauma triage people.
We wanted to get out front where we could
use our skills." —WILLIAM BROWN

"We triage the community as we go through—
situations that we can respond to, situations
we need to let go." —CHRIS ALBERTSON

"There were about 3,000 people there, including
firemen, policemen, nurses, and pharmacists.
They set up a triage unit and were able to
keep the peace intact." —CATHEY LEWIS

When we hear the word *triage*, most of us think of the process of sorting victims of a disaster or battle to determine medical priority. However, in the context of this chapter, I'll use the word to refer to the act of determining priorities that require action when it comes to the health of an existing church and creating the kind of margin that will enable the church to do what God calls it to do, when He says to do it.

As a pastor or ministry leader, you've already gained enough information to do an initial assessment of your priorities, processes, and procedures—with a little indirect hand holding from me. Let's start by taking a look at some of your church's numbers you'd like to change to find margin. You may have a spreadsheet that details your income and expense, or perhaps you use QuickBooks or another accounting software. Whatever you have, let's use that to start.

If you don't yet have this information organized, no worries. You can go back to chapter 9 and use that budget to help you create your own. The important step right now is that you have your numbers before you in a format that you can work with. I'm going to walk you through seven practical steps, some of which are similar to those in the previous chapter, that will enable you to change course and find margin in your finances.

STEP ONE: ASSEMBLE YOUR NUMBERS IN COLOR

I will stand my watch and set myself on the rampart, and watch to see what He will say to me, and what I will answer when I am corrected (HABAKKUK 2:1).

With your numbers before you, assembled with income at the top and expenses at the bottom, we'll begin the process of color-coding them. We want to properly assess the actual percentages of the budget allocated to the following four-category budget framework we established in chapter 9, along with desired percentages for optimal financial health:

- Giving...10%
- Savings 10%
- Employees and services 35%
- Ministry operations and building.................45%

STEP TWO: DO THE MATH

So teach us to number our days, that we may gain a heart of wisdom (PSALMS 90:12).

Everything on your income statement (P&L) should be marked with the color that designates it as belonging to one of the four budget categories. Let's say, for example, that you assigned yellow to the category of *giving*; therefore, you will also color code with yellow any dollar amount associated with giving. Repeat this process with the other three categories: *savings, employees and services,* and *ministry operations and building.* Once you've color-coded all your figures, add them together to determine the total dollar amount in each color-coded area. To convert these dollar amounts to percentages, refer to your current-year budget numbers.

Remember, the objective is to find margin in the budget; therefore, each year's budget is established at 90 percent of the previous year's income. If you've not already done so, take your previous year's total income and multiply it by 90 percent (.90). For example, if your total income last year was $220,000, then 90 percent of that dollar amount is $198,000; this is your total budget for the current year. The math equation looks like this: $220,000 x .90 = $198,000.

Now you can take your dollar totals for each category and convert them to actual percentages so that you can compare those percentages to your goal percentages. Let's say that your color-coded dollar amount in savings is $5,000. Dividing that figure by the budget figure we established in the previous paragraph, $198,000, gives you the percentage you're looking for. The math equation for this step looks like this: $5,000 ÷ $198,000 = .025; so the total percentage of your savings is 2.5 percent, which is under your goal of 10 percent savings by 7.5 percent.

By repeating this process for each of your four color-coded areas, you'll have a realistic perspective of your budget and a good foundation on which to establish your future goals. You'll need the help of a team of people who care about you and the church, some of whom have business and finance expertise. If you already have a board of trustees, start with these people. I recommend you do this sooner rather than later and that this team holds monthly meetings to ensure the church remains on track to pull ahead toward its newly established goals.

STEP THREE: REVIEW SALARIES AND
MAKE NECESSARY CHANGES

*And remain in the same house, eating and drinking
such things as they give, for the laborer is worthy of his
wages. Do not go from house to house* (LUKE 10:7).

Evaluating individual staff salary matrixes is the most effective
way to determine if you're heading the right direction with the
people you pay to perform the roles of ministry. A *salary matrix*
is a chart used to determine the annual salary award and rate of
salary progression of an individual employee.

If you determine you are paying people to perform tasks rather
than paying them to build volunteer teams, you'll need to make
some changes. This merely means modifying job descriptions in
a way that centers individuals on building teams.

Color-coding your overall salaries matrix will show you if
you're overspending in an area of ministry or not paying enough
attention to another, thus enabling you to make appropriate
changes. Data is the key to making the right calls and transitions,
so make sure you have clear and accurate data to measure. This
process is obviously not one to be shared with your staff, which
is why I recommend involving only your board of trustees. It's a
good thing to have highly involved trustees in your organization.

Should you determine changes or transitions are necessary
in staffing, make changes honorably and with plenty of advance
notice. How you treat people in these situations is of vital importance, for it will be a determining factor in how your staff views

you as a leader. If these changes require that someone leaves your organization, a financial investment into a severance package or a few weeks' paid transition time is a wise decision. It always pays to honor people, and any money spent to do so is never wasted money.

It's always best to revise job descriptions or transition staff members to areas better suited for their gifts and talents; however, such revisions and transitions are not always possible. Great leaders find a way to take the heat for difficult situations within their organizations. If you have to say goodbye to a member of your staff, apologize for not being clear about the job's requirements, and then let the rest of the staff know that in the coming weeks you'll be bringing more clarity about the organization and their roles, which they will have the opportunity to agree with or not.

Taking the heat for changes isn't easy, but it paves the way for any additional changes that need to be made at the time.

STEP FOUR: BREAK DOWN THE BUDGET TO MINISTRY AREAS

And God has appointed these in the church: first apostles, second prophets, third teachers, after that miracles, then gifts of healings, helps, administrations, varieties of tongues (1 CORINTHIANS 12:28).

By now you should have a good idea of how you want to handle the four color-coded categories of your budget. So it's time to evaluate each area of ministry and the funds staff members will have to work with in the upcoming year.

If you haven't already done so, the opportunity is at hand for you to develop staff members into "budget owners," making them responsible for their own line items. By involving them in creating their individual line items, giving them a say in the matter, they will buy into the process and work toward the overall goals you establish.

Work with your staff on their budgetary line items and create separate spreadsheets for each area of ministry that give a more detailed look at the budget for the year. Doing so will help keep your staff on track throughout the year because they will always have an updated view of their spending and where they are in their budgets.

At Grow Church the goal of every budget cycle, meaning the time between budget start and close annually (Grow Church's fiscal year is July 1 through June 30), is to have the directors in charge of budget line items evaluate their budgets based on a projected minimum of 10 percent growth for the upcoming year. This means they need to budget for *more* than 10 percent growth so that they have some margin in their line items. Doing so enables them to move around a bit during the year if prices go up or if better ideas come to light.

I've trained our directors to include a 5–10 percent margin in their budgets for safety throughout the year. Things are always changing in a growing church, and I want to ensure we can always say *yes* when presented with a great idea or opportunity. Margin gives us the ability to do so.

Our directors receive a monthly budget report so that they will always know the status of their budget lines. The report allows them to have full control as owners and prevents any surprises when it comes to their areas of ministry. Of course, we have in place a process of approvals for expenditures to ensure both directors and the church are protected as we operate within the budget.

Nobody ever goes over budget—ever! Those responsible for budget lines may make changes in their budgets (with approval from their supervisors) but they may not go over budget without the approval of the executive pastor. Our approval processes are in place to keep everyone safe—and they work.

STEP FIVE: ASSEMBLE THE CHURCH CALENDAR

Let all things be done decently and in order (1 CORINTHIANS 14:40).

At the time you are reading this book, your annual church calendar is probably already firmly in place, so instead of walking you through the process for your church, I'll let you glean insight from how Grow Church handles the relationship between its calendar and budget.

Our church calendar dictates our budget in that the calendar determines how we spend money to accomplish our clearly defined goals that represent our Big 4 mission components (see chapter 5). It's important that all directors buy off on the calendar so that they agree with resourcing from their areas of ministry and with the time constraints necessary to accomplish the calendar goals.

Because we consider our directors *owners,* we take one full day with them to prepare the annual calendar. These directors have already met with the staff members in their departments to assemble their departments' calendars for the year. Staff members know these calendars will likely be modified, but having their input is imperative for good morale on a church staff.

Completing the calendar requires numerous conversations, discussions, and challenges to ideas. Issuing challenges is the most productive tool in determining that every event fits into one of our Big 4 objectives. If an event doesn't fit, we remove it from the calendar.

When the calendar is set, we verify our budgets to ensure our budgeting is based on our objectives for the year. By involving the entire team of directors in this process, they will work together throughout the coming year for the "win," especially during times when teamwork is challenging.

Throughout most any year we have several initiatives or events that do not have a budget assigned to them. These are our "special-ticket events" paid for through ticket sales. Two such special-ticket events are our annual men's and women's events, for which we have a method for setting the ticket price.

We first determine how much it will cost to put on the event, and then we increase that figure by 10 percent to cover any unforeseen expenses. We know exactly how many people can be seated in our auditorium, so we take the projected cost of the event and divide it by the number of seats to determine the price of individual tickets.

If everything goes as planned and we don't have to utilize our 10 percent margin, we can put that money toward either next year's event or a missional initiative. In the beginning we were nervous about charging enough to cover the cost of our special-ticket events, but we've since learned that people are more than willing to pay for an event conducted with excellence. Excellent events fill future events because people will invite their friends to attend with them.

Our goal is to hear people say, "Wow! This church does everything with excellence." And that's exactly what they say about Grow Church events.

STEP SIX: HOW TO ANSWER QUESTIONS THAT DON'T HAVE DEFINITIVE ANSWERS

And He said to them, "It is not for you to know times or seasons which the Father has put in His own authority" (ACTS 1:7).

As pastors and church leaders, we are oftentimes faced with situations or circumstances not addressed in church policies and procedures. I'll use Grow Church as an example.

Our facility is ideally configured and located in a way that makes it appealing for usage by organizations outside the church; so several years ago we made the decision to rent our facility for outside events. You may say, "Wait a minute, Pastor James. I thought you didn't schedule any events that didn't fit into your Big 4 goals." This statement is correct; however, we knew by keeping our price slightly *below* competitive venues, we would gain great exposure in our community and thereby draw new people to the church. That's what happened, but we soon discovered that with the great exposure came a significant problem. It became taxing on our staff to schedule, set up, supervise, and tear down these outside events.

With no definitive guideline for this situation in our protocols and policies, we went back to our Big 4 criteria to challenge ourselves and see if we could make some adjustments in the way we managed these events to keep them in line with our goals. We firmly believed that exposing the community to Grow Church created opportunity to introduce people to Jesus, which after all is our primary goal; we just needed to make a slight course correction.

By upping our prices so that they were in line with those of similar venues in the area, we were able to hire competent people to staff and manage the events and still make money for the church. Grow Church now holds events that are a blessing to our community without putting any demand on our staff, which we consider a win-win.

We've learned when situations or questions arise that are outside policies and procedures, we simply process them through the lens of the Big 4. If something doesn't fit into the Big 4, it doesn't fit into our church.

STEP SEVEN: ESTABLISH A PROCESS FLOW FOR FIRST-TIME VISITORS

Then he brought them up into his house and set a meal before them. How he and his household rejoiced because all were now believers (ACTS 16:34 TLB).

First-time visitors at a church service, especially nonbelievers, should feel comfortable throughout the *entire* process, from the moment they step onto the church's property until they depart the property. The term *process flow* refers to the ease a first-time visitor experiences in finding where they need to go next. This need for ease is the reason it is vitally important you and your staff take a critical walk-through of everything that happens at your church on a Sunday morning.

You may wonder, *Why a Sunday morning?* Because that's where you'll find most of your first-time visitors. If you can see the experience through their eyes, you'll have the ability to make that experience exceptional for them. Because church experiences are as unique and varied as churches themselves, your Sunday morning walk-through will be entirely different from everyone else's. But to help you get into the mindset of a first-time visitor, here's a short list of questions to ask yourself:

- When approaching the church from the street, what do visitors see?

- Is the signage well placed, professional, and visible?

- When visitors drive onto the church property, how do they know where to go?

- How are visitors made to feel special while still in their vehicles?

- When visitors exit their vehicles, is someone there to walk them to the building and introduce them to a volunteer who can direct them according to their needs?

- If visitors have special needs (a child in a stroller or someone in a wheelchair), is a volunteer available to assist them?

Once inside the building, visitors should be able to easily identify volunteers who can answer questions and direct them. Our volunteers all wear prominent name tags, and many wear Grow Church tee shirts. My point is that visitors can easily find someone to answer their questions—usually without walking more than six feet! Do we expect our volunteers to have all the answers to every question? No, but they do understand and can communicate the basic Sunday-service process flow.

The list of questions below helped us create our own process flow. You may need to ask yourself different questions appropriate to your church; however, these questions will help you get started:

- Do visitors know we have special wheelchair seating on aisles for ease of getting in and out?

- Do parents with children know to turn left and drop off their kids first, prior to proceeding to the auditorium?

- Do parents know they are permitted in the children's ministry area, and that both they and their children will receive matching name tags?

- Do parents know their children are welcome to attend the adult service with them?

- Do nursing mothers know we have a special room for them?

- Do visitors know where the restrooms are located?

- Do visitors know they can meet with someone for personal prayer following the service, or purchase books and merchandise in the bookstore?

- Do first-time visitors know they are considered our VIPs, and we have a gift for them following the service?

- Do visitors know the lead pastors are available immediately after the service to meet them?

- If visitors are interested in baptism, taking part in a discipleship class, or taking the next step in connecting with the church, do they have the information they need to do so?

Again, this is not a comprehensive list of questions; rather, they are intended to help direct you in making your own process flow for your church. Once your process flow is in place, take the time to talk to visitors and ask if they are finding their way easily. Once you have a good process flow, be diligent to find ways to improve it. Thomas A. Edison, known throughout the world as America's greatest inventor, challenged his staff with this now-famous quotation: "There's always a way to do it better—find it!"

Make excellence your goal in everything connected with your services—from signage, to conversations, to announcements, to well-stocked restrooms—and then get your staff involved in finding ways to do it better. People love excellence, and they'll return to your church because of it.

———

Performing triage on your church doesn't have to be a messy endeavor, though doing so does require determination and commitment. The six practical steps I've outlined in this chapter will guide you safely to a place of peace and rest, secure in the knowledge that God's hand is upon you to grow a healthy church.

CHAPTER ELEVEN REVIEW:

1. It is imperative you take steps to gain financial control of your church.

   » **CHALLENGE:** This chapter may be your best resource out of all your resources so far. Consider using this chapter as a guide to establish your budget and gain back financial control of your organization.

2. Overall color coding of your budget, as well as your staff salaries, will help you understand where all your attention in the ministry is going.

   » **CHALLENGE:** Consider color coding salaries and employee benefits according to departments, so that you can get a clear look at where your employees/services funds are currently going. This will help you understand the future changes you need to make in your staffing.

3. Defining the clear purpose for each employee position is vital to your church's health.

   » **CHALLENGE:** Review and evaluate your employee job descriptions quarterly to make sure that roles haven't changed. If they have changed, this review will help you have a clear guide to what each employee is focusing on to help grow the church.

4. Your church calendar dictates the annual budget.

   » **CHALLENGE:** Consider taking one-to-two days with key staff members to complete the annual calendar prior to budgeting the upcoming year. This process is critical to meeting all goals for the ministry, and to ensure that you aren't cutting financial corners on annual events that carry out the church's purpose.

_____

_____

_____

_____

HOW TO PLANT A HEALTHY CHURCH

"Church planting teaches two things more than any other: that God is faithful and that we must learn how to depend on a faithful God." —CHRISTINE HOOVER

"If God only used perfect people, nothing would get done. God will use anybody if you're available." —RICK WARREN

"Plant the kind of church that you would want to be a part of even if you weren't the lead pastor." —ANSON MCMAHON

"Expect great things from God; attempt great things for God." —WILLIAM CAREY

I've written this chapter especially for those of you who are about to step into your calling from God and plant a church. I want to let you know how proud I am of you and your boldness to do what God is calling you to do. It takes a valiant person to do such, and for that, I am grateful for you. We need more people like you who are also willing to accept the calling and go forward without hesitation.

I am praying for you, though not by name, as I spend time in prayer frequently for pastors of new church plants. Yours is a calling that can be heavy at times, but God is faithful. You have the endurance necessary for this purpose, and the Holy Spirit will never let you down—even when the path before you gets challenging.

I remember my early years of church planting; we made so many mistakes. I thought that by this time I would be the expert in planting and growing healthy churches, but what I've learned with time is that every year there is so much more to learn and grow in. I want my failures and successes to be used for His glory, and I've written the material in this chapter from many failures God turned into successes. Grow Church is a combination of both, but in the end, God has created a healthy church through Tracy and me. We know that you can do it too because you have what it takes. So read on, and be encouraged through this road-map to success in building a healthy church from the ground up.

DETERMINING YOUR CHURCH'S FIRST-YEAR BUDGET

"Write the vision and make it plain on tablets, that he may run who reads it" (HABAKKUK 2:2).

Let's say you have data (or pro forma data, which is a hypothetical financial-figure estimate) that indicates your church will bring in $200,000 in the first year. To allow for sufficient margin, you would set your budget at 90 percent of that figure, or $180,000.

Here is how the four-category budget framework looks with percentages and dollar amounts:

- Giving 10% = ...$18,000
- Savings 10% =...$18,000
- Employees and services 35% = ... $63,000
- Ministry operations and building 45% = ...$81,000

As you can see, this budget breakdown doesn't allow for an adequate full-time staff, if these fictitious numbers were your actual numbers. So you'll likely need to start with part-time people to serve in the five most significant areas of ministry, which I consider to be (1) pastor/director, (2) children's director, (3) worship director, (4) production director, and (5) administrator. Because Tracy and I are business owners as well as being highly trained and experienced in all areas of ministry, we did not have to take salaries from the church when we filled its leadership gaps ourselves. As a result, the budget allowed more funds to go to staff support.

I'm certainly aware that many great churches started out with little more than a vision, faith, and virtually no money. I've also experienced the reality of the saying, "Where God guides, He provides." But on the basis of my business experience and the years I've spent as a pastor, I recommend that anyone who wants to start a church raise enough funds ahead of time to cover the first year's projected budget.

You may say, "Wow, Pastor James, that's an enormous amount of money to raise!" I agree; however, there are organizations that help pastors raise funds for startup churches. One such organization is the Association of Related Churches (ARC). They do a full analysis of the pastor and his or her spouse, the intended area for the church plant, and the possibility of sponsoring a portion of the launch budget.

Pastors who have a vision to launch a church understandably want to get started quickly; however, doing so is hardly ever the right approach. I make this statement on the basis of my personal experience as a man who likes to get things done, cast a vision, and then run toward it. There's a well-known statement in the carpentry trade that goes like this: measure twice, cut once. It means you should double-check your measurements before cutting a piece of wood so as not to waste time and material. My personality type much prefers to cut first and maybe measure along the way—but it's not a productive approach to anything.

I've learned if I will just slow down a bit, I'll have less challenges to deal with as I move steadily forward. Ultimately, taking the time to execute a strategic approach to any process, especially funding a church startup, will ultimately speed up the process.

Committing to a fundraising initiative prior to launching a church will help you formulate your team, strategize appropriately, and launch at the correct time of year for your geographical location. And yes, there most certainly is a correct time to launch a strategically assembled and healthy team.

What I mean by the *correct time* is that every geographic location has different seasons, different peak seasons of travel to and from, different climates, and other variables. You will want to know your area so well that you understand when people attend church the most. For example, in Naples, people are very transient in the summer. In August people get their schedules back in order for the start of the school year. However, we also have a seasonal community that visits the area from January through April. Therefore, the best time to launch a church in Naples would either be August or January to our estimation, and we've proven this concept over the past few years.

FUNDRAISING

The LORD said to Moses, "Tell the Israelites to bring me an offering. You are to receive the offering for me from everyone whose heart prompts them to give" (EXODUS 25:1–2 NIV).

The term *fundraise* can be a bit scary for any pastor or ministry leader, so I first want to define my use of the term as used in this section, and then give some practical examples of how to do it.

Though I will use the term *fundraising* in this section because it is understandable, I'm aware that in a church setting some people liken fundraising to having their pockets picked. As a pastor, I don't want to do to someone else anything that I wouldn't want done to me. For this reason, at Grow Church we have never done, nor will do, traditional fundraising events.

I do not consider myself a *fundraiser*; rather, I am a *vision caster*. Though the two terms may seem vastly different, in the context of starting a church, they are much the same. People don't fund someone else's plans for success—they fund vision. My experience has proven if a vision is clear and motivating, people will fund it.

Oftentimes young pastors come out of seminary with the idea that because they are willing and ready to preach, people will come to hear them. This is not usually the case.

Pastors of startup churches need to market their churches by getting out into the community and doing things not normal for church leaders. If you are getting ready to start a church, my advice is first to generate enough funds to support the first-year's budget prior to launching. If you can demonstrate the ability to generate funds for the startup of your church, you'll have confidence in your ability to generate funds as needed throughout the life of your organization.

But let me give you a word of warning: fundraising is most always a challenge to your vision (in a good way). People will sponsor a clear vision that aligns with their own personal vision and values. If at first they don't sponsor your vision, go back to the drawing board, clear up and simplify your vision, and continue to present it. You may need to repeat the process of refining your vision several times, but don't lose heart—people *will* start showing interest in your Spirit-led initiatives and want to take part in bringing them to pass.

The key to involving others in your vision is to learn to wrap your vision around the things they care about. People genuinely value matters that are important to them, and I've found these three are usually at the top of the list:

- Their families
- Their own success and future
- Their communities

Keeping these three values in mind, let's see how they fit into a vision-casting scenario in a way that allows people to fully buy in to that vision as they move from mere interest to full participation or sponsorship.

PARTICIPATION AND PARTNERSHIP

For we are fellow workmen (joint promoters, laborers together) with and for God (1 CORINTHIANS 3:9 AMPC).

When Tracy and I came to Naples to help the once small, struggling congregation that is now Grow Church, we first had to triage their situation and then make appropriate adjustments in the way they handled finances and ran the business side of the church. Once the organization was stable, Tracy and I knew the most effective way to move the church to a healthy position was to approach it as if it were a startup. Armed with a vision and a plan to get there, we went to work.

The way we got to know the people we met within our new community was to invite them to dinner at our home. There, in an unhurried and intimate setting, we could ask them thoughtful questions about who they were and what was important to them. These were people we met at the gym, the supermarket, at the Christian bookstore, and even at church.

We wanted to create relationships, so oftentimes at the beginning of our evening together, we'd ask our guests, "What's your dream?" This question is my wife's go-to question, and it works marvelously to get people talking. Most people are taken aback by this question and need time to process before answering, so we'd proceed with simpler topics, including the three listed in the previous section. It was more important to Tracy and me to create relationships by learning about other people's interests rather than trying to interest them in our initiatives. Building relationships in this manner occurred only because we were genuinely interested in the people we met with—a prerequisite for successful pastoring.

We found once we got to know various individuals and what was important to them, including their own dreams, it was easy to cast vision and then watch them move from being interested in our vision into full participation and partnership with that vision. The vision ends up being their vision as well, if you listen well.

Using each of the values listed in the previous section, *family, personal success and future,* and *community,* here are three scenarios of what this process looks like:

Community. Let's say you find out the couple you're developing relationship with has a dream to feed the less fortunate people in the community, perhaps the homeless or those who struggle with addiction. We know Jesus Himself fed the hungry, so it's only natural to agree with this biblical practice. Let the couple know how their dream lines up with your vision. If you plan to have a feeding outreach in your community, tell them so. If not, let them know of any local organizations you support as they work to end hunger in your area. In so doing, you've found the couple's passion point and answered it with your vision regarding transformation of your community in the area that means the most to them. Making this connection between their passion and your vision is the first step.

We don't want any family to go without positive influence and help, in raising their kids and establishing success in their families.

The next step in moving people into participation and partnership is to share a sneak peek at how things will look when your startup church begins to grow. For instance, you can tell people your church will give 10 percent to missions, as well as partner with the hurting in your city, with a goal of securing a large amount of sponsorship at the end of year one. Be ready to provide numbers from your pro forma and financial goals. Remember, you are casting vision.

As Tracy and I became more proficient in relationship building and casting vision, we found we never had to ask people if they wanted to participate; rather, they initiated questions about how they could get involved. For this reason I advise pastors and leaders of startup churches to make it a practice *not* to ask people to participate. If you cast the vision effectively, they will want to join you in seeing that it comes to pass, which means you've likely just landed a volunteer-team member who may also be a financial sponsor in the future.

Healthy fundraising begins with building relationships and finding common goals, and then inviting those you are in relationship with to attend an upcoming interest-group meeting, which I'll describe later in this chapter, with other people who also want to change the community or city.

Personal success and future. Let's say the next person you have dinner with tells you he or she dreams of being the biggest influencer in the city, owning the biggest business, and sponsoring major projects to help kids without families. That single statement reveals opportunities to connect to your vision for the city, that there will be no family-less kids. But this individual gave you some other clues as well: he or she is interested in becoming all God has called him or her to be.

How do people become all they can be? They need others to help them, a group of people who will encourage, uplift, and stand strong with them. They need people who believe in them. They need to serve alongside others who want the same things for their city and to rub shoulders with other local business owners to make each other strong. What better place to find these relationships than a local church with both a missional mindset and the belief in the God-given gifts inside each person—a church built upon people's gifts rather than upon filling the needs of the church with whoever shows up.

If an individual connects with the vision, let him or her know about the upcoming interest-group meeting.

Grow Church is a gift-based church, which means we honor the God-given gifts in those He sends to us. We've designed a system that identifies the gift and then helps individuals make a difference with their gifts (see chapter 8). It's obvious the person described above has a gift of leadership, so it would be good to cast some vision about how he or she could be used to further the kingdom of God and lead others in using those gifts to change the community as well.

> *Never try to make money; instead, meet a need and the money will come.*

Family. Finally, you meet a couple whose commitment is first and foremost to their family. This doesn't mean they are concerned for their family only; rather, it means they have huge hearts for families in general—though they might not yet know it. As you purpose to build relationship with this couple, you can direct the conversation to dreaming about helping other families become healthy and whole. You can cast vision for raising kids with a biblical world view and for a state-of-the-art children's ministry that makes kids wake their parents each Sunday morning to go to church.

If as some say, it takes a village to raise a child, at Grow Church we want to be that village. We don't want any family to go without positive influence and help, in raising their kids and establishing success in their families. Far too many bad influences exist in the world, so teaching kids at a young age how to serve or demonstrating how to discuss Bible verses at the dinner table are just a few ways we can begin to change a community.

If you're excited about this couple's interests because yours are the same, they will be excited about what you want to do in their community and will likely ask you how they can get involved. That's a great time to tell them about the interest-group meeting you are planning.

Here are five key points to remember when starting a new church:

- Get out into your community and create relationships.
- Show you are truly interested in individuals. This interest is something that can't be faked.
- Find their interests in your vision.
- Talk about how their interests align with yours and how you can change the world together.

Generating funds for a startup church doesn't need to involve hype, traditional promotional efforts, or cajoling people to support your plans. Generating funds is a natural byproduct of the local church simply *being* the church prior to its official opening.

It's finding common ground, casting vision, connecting others' interests to your vision, and then allowing them to partner with that vision.

I like this statement, which applies to both business and church: Never try to make money; instead, meet a need and the money will come.

CONTINUE TO CAST VISION

> Write the vision and engrave it so plainly upon tablets that everyone who passes may [be able to] read [it easily and quickly] as he hastens by (HABAKKUK 2:2 AMPC).

The kind of vision casting described in the previous section will never end in your church; you'll find that you are always casting vision. People who bring money are merely setting the pace for your vision, but they won't bring their money unless your vision sets them on fire to do something.

We continue to cast vision at Grow Church, though the process is a little different than when we began. At that time, we were casting vision with little to show for it and working to get people to come to our interest-group meetings, yet we are doing somewhat the same thing today. Since Grow Church has set a precedent for generosity through our missions-giving strategy and our serve events, when there is a need, it is usually already met or being served by our church. The reason needs are met is that people have already been positioned to sow generously into missions so it doesn't take the normal "ask" to gain their financial support. You can expect similar future results in your ministry by setting a culture of generosity from the onset.

I've been asked many times, "Pastor James, what is Grow Church working on right now?" That's usually code for, "How can I get involved financially?" I always have a million-dollar project in mind to share with people who ask this question, as well as a list of projects we want to accomplish in the next year or two. I've trained our staff to do the same thing because, due to the exponential growth at Grow Church, people often approach staff members with these questions, and the staff needs to be ready to answer.

When recently asked about our current project, I said, "We're working toward a $100,000 gift to a local shelter that is doing a building project." The gentleman I was talking with said, "Well, how about I give half that amount?" Of course, I thanked him for his generosity and gladly accepted his gift.

I remember the time when someone requested to have coffee with the executive pastor (me), which usually means there's either a big problem or a big gift coming our way. In this case it was a gift, and the individuals first wanted to understand a little more about some vision casting we'd done. It turned out they sponsored a massive amount of our annual end-of-year giving initiatives.

A time will never exist that you're not in need of funds, and the way to generate them is by casting enough big vision for people to get behind it. When they do, their giving will accelerate the pace of the vision.

Before we move on from the topic of generating funds, I want to cast vision for your church's future by sharing how we recognize and honor those who have a gift of giving. These amazing individuals are known as our Legacy Team.

LEGACY TEAM

Having then gifts differing according to the grace that is given to us, let us use them: ... he who gives, with liberality (ROMANS 12:6, 8).

In about year six following the startup of Grow Church, we instituted an idea we got from Church of the Highlands and started a Legacy Team.

Establishing this team in affluent southwest Florida was not difficult, for many people who live here have been greatly blessed by God in their businesses and finances, and they love being a blessing to their church and other community initiatives. We also have people who live here during the winter season, whom we refer to as our "snowbirds." They have a home church in the city where they reside, but they make Grow Church their church while they reside in Naples each winter.

Once or twice each year we host a Legacy Team dinner in honor of these individuals who so love to be a blessing and give. The purpose of the dinner is not to ask for money; rather we cast vision by sharing some of those audacious goals that Tracy and I establish for Grow Church each January. These meetings are some of the most fun and enjoyable events we hold, for the attendees enjoy engaging with the vision of Grow Church and then having the opportunity to help make that vision come to pass. We've learned that big givers need big vision—and that is what we always cast at Grow Church.

INTEREST-GROUP MEETINGS

"Come, follow me," Jesus said, "and I will send you out to fish for people." At once they left their nets and followed him (MATTHEW 4:18 NIV).

An interest-group meeting is just what its name suggests, a meeting of people from your local area who have shown interest in your church launch. For them to have shown interest means you have already connected with them somewhere or they have come to dinner at your home.

Though we didn't feel it necessary to run ads on social media, doing so is a viable way to invite people to learn about the launch of a new church that will bring life to the community. If you decide to use social media, give yourself a runway of at least two months to create in-person relationship with those who respond before holding the meeting.

You should not hold your first interest-group meeting until a minimum of ten people have committed to attend, which means you'll probably need to invite fifteen. Having ten attendees ensures enough people in the room to generate energy and ask the kind of questions that build positive anticipation about the church launch. An effective way to increase participation at your interest-group meeting is to ask those who plan to attend to bring someone who might also be interested. Any individual who brings another person should be identified as a possible leader capable of helping you evangelize your city.

When we held our initial interest-group meetings, we purposed to keep the agenda simple with only five activities:

- **PRAYER**: Nothing happens without prayer; therefore, prayer must be the foundation on which every aspect of any church is established.

- **CAST VISION**: The vision should be larger than what just a few individuals can handle on their own. It should require miraculous intervention to accomplish, including more people and resources than are currently available. Big vision creates a sense of excitement in those who are part of it.

- **FORESHADOW UPCOMING EVENTS**: We found that one of the most effective tools in preparing for a successful launch was to schedule community outreach events prior to the launch. It's amazing what God can accomplish with a small group of people who have the faith to make a big impact by serving at a local food pantry or any one of dozens of established, credible community outreaches. Outreaches of this nature are a great way for a startup church to demonstrate that it is there for the community.

- **ENCOURAGE INVITATIONS TO OUTREACH EVENTS:** Outreach events are a great way to involve others in serving their communities. We make it a point to tell interest-group meeting attendees to invite a friend to help them serve, because we've learned that people who serve frequently attend subsequent interest-group meetings. Outreach events also give us the opportunity to invite those whom we serve to an interest-group meeting.

- **GET TO KNOW PEOPLE PERSONALLY:** Relational equity will play a huge part in your success. Though getting to know someone personally takes time, the objective is to be vulnerable. People want to know their pastors will do anything for them and for the community. They need to know what makes their pastors tick and about their pastor's family. They need to see their pastors demonstrate servant leadership, which means their pastors won't tell them to do anything they don't also do.

Once you've achieved momentum, have monthly interest-group meetings for a period of six months, which will give you time to build your necessary volunteer teams in preparation for the church launch. To ensure team members' optimal effectiveness in the areas where they serve requires you know each person intimately. For example, you should know their skill sets, personality types, what they like, and which area of ministry they enjoy most.

After you've completed a few interest-group meetings, you'll be ready to schedule more detailed team meetings to determine where people will serve in the upcoming church launch. Once you match people to their area of service, then they can assist you in assembling the processes involved with that area of ministry.

The people who come out of interest-group meetings and into team meetings are those who have taken hold of the vision and are ready to implement the systems that will get you to launch day.

FIRST-YEAR BUDGET BREAKDOWN (NOT INCLUDING STARTUP BUDGET)

*Be diligent to know the state of your flocks, and
to attend to your herds* (PROVERBS 27:23).

Though raising initial funds to cover a first-year budget is a huge responsibility and will take more time to accomplish than you may like, if you follow the advice in this chapter, you'll likely be thankful for it. There's nothing more burdensome for a church than to depend on the weekly offering to pay the bills. This kind of dependence creates unnecessary pressure on both the church staff and the attendees, and it will ultimately scare people away. Having the first-year's budget in the bank allows a church to launch without the pressure of finances.

In our following hypothetical situation, which is based on one of Grow Church's original budgets, we've established the first-year budget at $180,000. Here's what that Grow Church budget looks like in spreadsheet form:

MINISTRY OPERATIONS AND BUILDING

CHURCH BUDGET		
	ANNUAL EXPENSES	TOTAL BUDGET $180K 90% of expectation
Church Planting	$3,500.00	
Human Trafficking Partnerships	$3,500.00	GIVING / MISSIONS
Bibles in Local Jails	$2,000.00	$18,000.00
Local Pantry	$5,400.00	Goal: (10% = $18,000)
Benevolence	$1,800.00	
Marginal Tragedy Relief	$1,800.00	
	$18,000.00	
		SAVINGS
	$18,000.00	Goal: (10% = $18,000)
	$18,000.00	
Event Planning / Mobile Church Admin	$5,040.00	EMPLOYEES & SERVICES
Administrator	$10,800.00	$66,288.00
Hispanic Ministry Admin	$1,200.00	Goal: (35% = $63,000)
Children Visuals	$5,040.00	
Payroll & Tax Expense	$3,312.00	
Children's Director	$2,400.00	
Sunday / Thurs Childcare	$6,000.00	
Cleaning Service Sunday	$6,960.00	
Cleaning Service Thurs and Admin	$10,416.00	
Worship Leader	$2,400.00	
Hispanic Ministry Pastor	$3,000.00	
Campus Setup Thurs / Sundays	$2,880.00	
Family Pastors	$5,040.00	
Maintenance	$1,800.00	
	$66,288.00	
UTILITIES		
Electric	$1,200.00	OPERATIONS & BLDG
Phone / Cable	$804.00	$77,644.00
SUPPLIES		(45% = $81,000)
Hospitality	$6,600.00	
Maintenance	$3,000.00	
Office Supplies	$8,500.00	
Technical	$3,600.00	
Special Events / Creative Arts	$360.00	
Administration	$3,600.00	
MINISTRIES		
Hispanic Ministry	$600.00	
Children's Ministry	$2,040.00	
Students	$900.00	
RENT		
Church Facility Sundays	$24,200.00	
Student Facility Weekly	$6,240.00	
College 2nd Facility for Classroom Space	$6,000.00	
Administrative Offices	$10,000.00	
	$77,644.00	**$179,932.00**

It's important to note that this setup follows the foundational Give-Save-Live principle established in chapter 7. Giving and saving appear at the very top of this budget because these two categories of the budget framework are of vital importance when stewarding money, both personal and for the church. Now let's take a closer look at the four categories in our sample budget.

GIVING

> *Each of you should give what you have decided in your heart to give, not reluctantly or under compulsion, for God loves a cheerful giver* (2 CORINTHIANS 9:7 NIV).

By placing *giving* first in your budget, you invite God's continual involvement in your finances. You *need* God's involvement in your budget, and when you honor Him, He will honor your work.

The 10 percent giving goal of the budget won't add up to 10 percent of actual income; it didn't for us because our actual income was more than projected. To ensure we didn't fall behind in our giving, we established two special times of yearly giving to "catch up" on our giving in relation to the church's actual income. One of these times is at the end of each calendar year, which is a great time to be generous during the holidays; the other is at the close of our fiscal year, June 30. At these times we look at our income and then adjust our giving as planned to a minimum 10 percent of actual income.

SAVINGS

The wise store up choice food and olive oil, but
fools gulp theirs down (PROVERBS 21:20 NIV).

A good savings plan for both personal and business budgeting is 10 percent, but the same is true for churches. Without savings, a startup church will not be positioned to purchase a building in the future with a required minimum of 30 percent down.

The more a church saves, the more it can influence its community. The more money a church saves, the lower its payment will be when it is time to purchase a building. A healthy savings account positions a church to be a greater blessing in the future. It is critical for any church that desires growth to establish and maintain a strong savings account.

EMPLOYEES AND SERVICES

Whatever you do, work at it with all your heart, as working
for the Lord, not for human masters (COLOSSIANS 3:23 NIV).

Keep in mind that the sample budget we are looking at is specific to Grow Church, and we did not initially have any employee benefits. Therefore, we chose to direct finances to meet distinct needs within our church.

Because Grow Church is in southwest Florida, we have a heavy Hispanic influence in our church family, which is why we directed funds to that area of ministry.

You will also notice that our actual budget of $66,288 was over the goal budget of $63,000 by a total of $3288. You too will likely go over budget in the beginning, and I want to assure you, it's nothing to go crazy about. Keep in mind that goals are just that—goals. Though they should be respected, they are intended to be guidelines that you work on each year until your actual numbers come into alignment with the goals. (Besides, you'll notice that we made up the difference in the section below.)

MINISTRY OPERATIONS AND BUILDING

"And I tell you that you are Peter, and on this rock I will build my church, and the gates of Hades will not overcome it" (MATTHEW 16:18 NIV).

When we launched Grow Church, we were what some refer to as a "setup/teardown" church. Another term is a "load-in/load-out" church, which means we rented time at multiple locations to accomplish our necessary meetings and events each week. Every event needed additional time to set up and tear down, time that needed to be allotted for.

Hospitality was a significant budget item in the beginning (and remains so today). We wanted to establish a church where everyone would feel welcome, could always have a beverage (mostly coffee) in their hands, and at all times know that someone cared for them.

When it comes to church operations, people will recognize what you value by where you spend your money.

Creating a church budget is the quickest way to get established in the path of effective stewardship. If you start this way and hold your ground, you'll always have enough money to cover needs when they arise. Remember: *margin* gives you the ability to do what God says to do, when He says to do it.

Most pastors and leaders don't understand the importance of establishing savings and margin *prior* to starting a church. When any church is in its fledgling state, resources are usually sparse, and need is great, I've found most of those who start without the precedent of margin (90 percent of the previous year's income or projected first-year's income) and savings never go back and establish it later. So be courageous and hold your ground where your budget is concerned. Fight off the urge to spend your margin now—and later you'll be pleased that you did.

STARTUP BUDGET BREAKDOWN

A man's heart plans his way, but the LORD directs his steps (PROVERBS 16:9).

We've assessed our hypothetical first-year's budget at $180,000, which means that's what it will take to run all operations, including facility rental, giving, and saving. But the first-year's budget is not the startup budget.

A startup budget consists of the one-time costs necessary to get the church started. Assemble these separate from your first-year budget so that they don't carry into your second-year budget.

Startup costs are heavily dependent on the type of facility you move into. For instance, if you start out in an existing church space or auditorium that already has live venues, you won't need to purchase much equipment and technology. However, if your startup location is a cafeteria or gym, you'll need all the technology, equipment, trucks, trailers, and signage to do a complete weekly setup/teardown of the facility. There are many differences in launches depending on the location, so let's look at examples of both these scenarios, existing space and cafeteria/gym, to see what a startup budget might look like.

Let's start with a church or auditorium space with existing equipment. You'll have to train people to operate the equipment, but ideally these individuals will be volunteers. Below is a sample budget for this scenario:

STARTUP BUDGET

(church or auditorium space with no technology purchase needed)

AREA	TOTAL AMOUNT
Security Deposit	$5,000.00
Marketing	$15,000.00
Computer / Tech	$3,000.00
Signage	$10,000.00
Team Supplies	$5,000.00
Worship	$2,000.00
Kids Check-In	$5,000.00
TOTAL STARTUP BUDGET	**$45,000.00**

The total startup budget number will be added into your first-year budget for a total overall figure. So, if your first-year budget is $180,000 and then you add the $45,000 (startup), your total overall figure is $225,000. But remember, you don't have to generate these funds by traditional fundraising—they will come to you through strategic and effective vision casting.

Much of your startup budget consists of the capital investments or supplies necessary to get your church off the ground and started, after which your annual budget kicks in and you'll have a monthly allocation for these items as they depreciate or need to be replaced. So your $45,000 startup budget comes prior to your church's generating any income following your vision casting (fundraising) efforts prior to launch.

Now let's look at a realistic startup budget for a church launch using a cafeteria or gymnasium space. The numbers are from Grow Church's launch of its first additional church location in the auditorium of a local technical college. Though the numbers are higher than reasonable for an initial church launch (remember, we're backed by years of effective budgeting, margin building, and savings) it gives clear detail of the areas to be funded. And with a little simple math, you can determine the percentages of the budget allocated to each area.

This budget requires more equipment than for an existing church space (including chairs, speakers, acoustic panels, wall dividers) and technology, as well as the means to transport these items to and from the location. You'll also need an additional team of volunteers to perform load in/load out services at the location. (This team is truly the most important team in this situation.)

STARTUP BUDGET

(cafeteria or gym)

AREA	TOTAL AMOUNT
Security Deposit	$5,000.00
Marketing	$15,000.00
Production	$150,000.00
Computers	$15,000.00
Lobby	$30,000.00
Signage	$12,000.00
Teams	$10,000.00
Worship	$1,000.00
Nursery / Preschool	$10,000.00
Elementary	$8,000.00
Kids Check-In	$8,000.00
Storage	$4,000.00
Vehicles and Trailers	$40,000.00
TOTAL STARTUP BUDGET	**$308,000.00**

Most of the areas listed on the left in the two versions of startup budgets are self-explanatory, but four need further definition.

Marketing efforts include several processes to ensure that everyone within a minimum ten-mile radius knows the church is there. Studies show that individuals must hear any given marketing message fifteen times before they act on it, so the goal is to send the message as many times and ways as possible.

Direct mail, specifically post cards, is one way to connect with people. The post card should be colorful, attractive, and large enough to stand out in a handful of mail. It needs an attention-grabbing headline such as "This piece of mail could change your life," and then on the back have benefit-driven copy that explains how being part of the church will do just what the head-line says. Look for a local company that specializes in direct mail to help you with both design and mailing.

You'll get the biggest bang for your buck with direct mail and social media.

Social media is another effective marketing tool. Simply post-ing is not enough, so spend some money on targeted marketing to the demographic you want to attract to your church. Facebook demographics are specific, helpful, and work well. Make sure you are not just promoting your church but letting the community know how the church will impact their needs or desires. You will need to know your local area's "pain points" to effectively minis-ter to them via marketing materials. Knowing *pain points* means understanding what the families in your local area are in need of, what types of issues need to be resolved, what families are experiencing economically, and any other needs your local area has or feels. Many of these pain points are common to every city in America, but some will be specific to your area. For example, in Naples, Florida, people experience pain points in relocating since our city is a highly sought-after place to live. This gives us the opportunity to speak directly to the hardship of finding a school for the kids or finding community in a new area.

Radio and television advertising works well in some locales, but it is expensive. You'll get the biggest bang for your buck with direct mail and social media.

Production includes all the necessary technology including audio boards, speakers, screens, projectors, cables, staging, backdrops, lighting, and other such items. This expense is most always the largest in today's world where people are conditioned to equate excellent sight and sound with credibility. The quality of production will either make you look and sound good, or it will do the opposite. Don't skimp on the quality of production or underestimate its ability to affirm your credibility.

Lobby expenses include signage, backdrops, popup signs, iPads for data entry or bookstore sales, sitting areas, coffee tables, and coffee stations, to name a few. Signage (which begins in the parking lot) is crucial so that people know from the moment they pull onto the property where they need to go. Once inside, they need to know how to find the children's ministry, the coffee station, restrooms, and of course the auditorium or sanctuary. Newcomers' having to ask is great when it comes to your making a personal connection with them; however, their asking is an indication your signage may be insufficient.

A church launch in a cafeteria or gym can be accomplished with a smaller budget ...

Teams refers to the expenses necessary to support the operation of the volunteer teams that serve during services. Such items may include parking lot vests, glow sticks, breakfast and/or lunch, tools for setup, handout materials, shirts, pens, iPads for data entry, cameras for the photography team, tape, nails, adhesive, TV for presenting information, and Apple TV for presentation. This line-item expense covers anything a team might need.

At Grow Church we like to launch every endeavor in the biggest way possible, but as I said, we are now an established church with a healthy budget. A church launch in a cafeteria or gym can be accomplished with a smaller budget, but whatever the total budget number is, it will be added to the first-year budget for a combined total first-year budget.

Some pastors are comfortable launching their churches with six months' expenses in the bank. Doing so certainly enables them to launch quicker and start generating income sooner. Each pastor and each church situation is different; the bottom line is that each should have peace about his or her decisions. The scenarios I've presented are designed to take away as much stress as possible during a church launch, but each pastor must decide what is best for him or her.

BUILDING TEAMS OF VOLUNTEERS

From him the whole body, joined and held together by every supporting ligament, grows and guilds itself up in love, as each part does its work (EPHESIANS 4:16 NIV).

When preparing to launch a startup church, people resources are equally important as financial resources.

I recommend having enough people on each volunteer team, including leaders, to cover the first three months following the church launch. Depending on how your organization is structured, these teams might include children's ministry, worship team, greeters, ushers, prayer partners, parking lot directors, and information booth support, to name a few.

From the beginning, Grow Church has had a VIP team in place for first-time guest assimilation. When someone new comes to the church, we want them to feel comfortable, direct them around the facility, and connect with them on a personal level. We also get their contact information and give them a special gift.

Build the team by matching individuals' interests and gifts with the church's needs.

It is imperative that a startup church have both a worship team and children's ministry team in place before launching; again, these teams should have enough people to fulfill the church's volunteer needs for the first three months. Some teams may require only one leader and one team member, but others will need more. For instance, your children's team will need one or two volunteers per room, and your worship team should have a minimum of two vocalists and three instrumentalists. If volunteers are unable to serve every week for the first ninety days, you may need to double the amount of team members to ensure adequate volunteer coverage during that period.

As you take into account your specific community and its unique demographics, you'll be able to pinpoint your needs for your launch. For example, your young adults' team can probably wait—unless you launch in a college town and expect much of your growth to come from that demographic.

I recommend you start building your team as far in advance of your launch as possible—six months at a minimum and one year at best. This approach will allow sufficient time for your face to get into the community to cast vision and grow a following.

You're probably thinking, *Wait a minute, Pastor James, how do I build teams of people before the church launches?* You will start with your lead team, which comes from the people in your community you first developed relationships with. These are individuals who attended your interest-group meetings and said yes to the vision you cast. These are people who want to serve and sow into that vision.

Once you identify these individuals, you involve them in monthly or weekly meetings to build your teams. Some will be interested in participating at different levels, so it's important to identify if they prefer to lead a team, serve on a team, or simply attend services. It's okay for people to do as little or as much as they like, but you need to know what you're working with to build the appropriate teams prior to launch.

Be clear in these team meetings about the number of people you need on each team prior to launch. Continue to cast vision and encourage your lead team to build their volunteer teams as you work together to get to your goals and launch well.

So the process of team building (at any level) looks like this:

- Have dinner or coffee to establish relationship and cast vision.

- Invite individuals to an interest-group meeting to connect with others and get more detailed information.
- Build the team by matching individuals' interests and gifts with the church's needs.

Now that your leadership team and initial volunteer teams are in place, you can prepare to grow these teams. Let's assume you launch your church with four hundred people in attendance the first Sunday. The number of people at a church launch usually dwindles to about half that number in attendance after four weeks. So at the end of the first month, you should have a solid two hundred people attending each week, and from these attendees you will build your volunteer teams. Again, marketing toward a launch weekend of four hundred people is a hypothetical scenario; you can decide the number you are reaching for.

We've determined that, for Grow Church, it takes about 20 percent of our attendance number to adequately serve at each service. Therefore, two hundred attendees will require around forty volunteers. We want people to feel well supported from the moment they arrive and throughout the whole service experience; this is the reason building teams is critical prior to launch.

———

Church planter, I know I've given you a lot of information that may *seem* like a very big mountain in front of you. My intention in writing this chapter is not to discourage you in the least; rather, it is to give you some handles on how you can adequately prepare for what God intends to do through you.

You are called by God for such a time as this. When you decide to step out by faith, you will see that God steps out with you. If you are making preparation to obey Him, He will lead you with His perfect wisdom. You can use this chapter as a either a guide or a reference to challenge your thinking. I would rather you be led by God instead of me as you prepare for the launch He is calling you to pursue.

Remember, it is His church, and He cares about it more than any human does. When you step out by faith, He will be sure to take you the rest of the way. Being strategic in your planning is another way of honoring God with His church and the finances He pours into it.

I believe and declare that your best days are in front of you and that God will support every directive you encounter along the way.

1. Fundraising provides a "sneak peek" of how your vision is being accepted by your community.

   » **CHALLENGE:** I know, fundraising is a challenge; however, it will be a necessary tool for growth for the rest of your days of leading church. Think about fundraising as casting vision. Consider planning a vision-casting event in the near future.

2. Finding the values of your local community is the best way to start casting vision particular to their interests.

   » **CHALLENGE:** Your community might be different than mine, and I hope you get to know members of your community well enough to understand what their interests are. Gaining this perspective will help you meet their interests within your vision casting, and you'll soon have enough volunteers and givers to accomplish more than ever before.

3. The key question to all people is this: What's your dream?

   » **CHALLENGE:** Do you know the dreams of your original start-up volunteer team members? If you know their dreams, you can help them accomplish those dreams through the local church, your church.

4. The Legacy Team sets the pace, but you set the vision.

   » **CHALLENGE:** Consider starting a Legacy Team to fund the vision that God put in your heart for your community, to be carried out through the local church. In your first meeting, you might want to plan on the following layout:

   - What the church did last year.
   - What the church is currently doing.
   - What the church's dreams are to change your community.

   _____

   _____

   _____

ADDENDUM: CHAPTER 9

A SAMPLE GROW CHURCH BENEFIT PACKAGE

When we created our first benefit package, it didn't contain everything we now provide for our staff. Our package is always growing and changing, which means it will look different with each year, but below is a list of benefits to use as guide for creating and growing a benefit package to honor your staff members.

HEALTH INSURANCE COVERAGE OF 75 PERCENT

- We want our staff to have the coverage they need. We are competitive in the current market, yet we continually evaluate the budget to make improvements as we grow.

401(K) SAVINGS PLAN MATCHING UP TO 3 PERCENT

- We teach our staff that there is no good reason for them not to contribute at least 3 percent, which in turn sets them up for 6 percent retirement savings.

CELL-PHONE ALLOWANCE

- This benefit is on an "as needed" basis for those who are required to be available by phone regularly for church business.

GYM MEMBERSHIP

- We believe in the "whole person" approach to health—spirit, soul, and body. Physical exercise is a big part of this value; therefore, we honor the temple of God by sponsoring it.

LIFELOCK PROTECTION

- Identity theft can take months to clear up, and during that time victims oftentimes experience untold stress. Providing this benefit ensures our staff members are protected.

SHORT-TERM DISABILITY

- This benefit covers most anything the health program misses, including a leave of absence for specific covered circumstances.

ACCIDENT PROTECTION

- Accidents happen from time to time, and our staff members have peace in knowing they are protected should they have an accident outside of church.

HOSPITAL-OVERAGE PROTECTION

- This benefit helps should a staff member have to remain in the hospital for longer than the normal insurance coverage time.

FIFTEEN "PERSONAL TIME OFF" (PTO) DAYS PER YEAR WITH TWENTY DAYS OFF AFTER FIVE YEARS

- Staff members' rest and relaxation are essential to a strong and healthy working environment in the business world. Therefore, we also give our church staff enough time off to stay fresh.

FOUR SICK DAYS PER YEAR

- We don't want staff members using their PTO days when they are sick, so we added some sick days to the package.

ONE PTO MISSION TRIP (SEVEN DAYS)

- Participating in a mission trip is as much a benefit to staff members as it is to those who are served on the mission field, which is the reason we sponsor one trip each year with additional personal time off.

$1,800 IN CONTINUING EDUCATION PER YEAR

- Readers are learners, and learners are earners. We've learned that a growing staff is a capable staff, and knowledge helps them stay on the cutting edge of their individual job assignments within the church.

- We sponsor one conference per year that usually requires our traveling outside our geographic area to participate in team-building activities together.

HOLDING COMPANY

We've set up an effective safety feature for our organization so that if anything such as a lawsuit came against the church posing a threat to our financial safety, our reserves and assets would be safe. After all, Jesus said, *"Behold, I send you out as sheep in the midst of wolves. Therefore be wise as serpents and harmless as doves. But beware of men, for they will deliver you up to councils and scourge you in their synagogues"* (Matthew 10:16–17).

We created a 501(c) (2) organization that acts as our holding company, a place where we store assets such as excess funds, buildings, property, and stocks. A holding company is a business entity that doesn't conduct any business activity; rather, it owns the assets that have been swept into it, and it has the ability to purchase other facilities for the church if the board approves. Holding companies protect their subsidiaries from financial losses because they cannot be pursued by creditors.

Our holding company is a safe place because it is a separate entity with a separate board of trustees. I am the only person on both the holding company board and the church board. The holding company board is kept up to speed on the assets in the holding company so that they can make wise investment decisions with the funds and property held there. For instance, the board may decide to create a *cash sweep* account instead of a normal savings account to ensure all the money and holdings in the account are federally insured by the FDIC.

It is important that the holding company's board members are experienced and knowledgeable when it comes to standard banking, accounting, finance, and business practices. Our members are well versed in these practices; they were selected because of their backgrounds in these fields.

Our church building, land, and all assets valued over $2,500 are on the holding company's balance sheet. They are not Grow Church assets; the holding company owns them.

Here's how our holding company works on behalf of Grow Church: As a 501(c) (3) tax-exempt organization the church maintains an operating account designated for day-to-day operations. We deposit all weekly giving income into this account, where we leave it to ensure all monthly expenses are covered with a little bit of margin. We keep $100,000 in the church's savings account as margin for anything that might pop up unexpectedly, such as repair of an air conditioning unit. Any funds that come in above what we keep in these two accounts are "swept" into the holding company for safekeeping.

The holding company now owns the assets swept into it and, with board approval, can make purchases on behalf of the church. The holding company's board can be removed or disbanded by the church board at any time; however, the holding company must at all times maintain a separate board because it is a separate entity.

ENDOWMENT

Grow Church has set up an endowment for future scholarships to our *Bloom Day School* for children and our adult *Grow School of Ministry*, as well as other Christian education initiatives that we may embark on in the coming years.

An *endowment* is an account or fund invested by an entity to support its educational mission through somewhat normalized annual returns. Out of that return, a percentage of the funds pays the tuition for those in need. Endowments are set up in perpetuity, which means they never go away.

Here's an example of how an endowment works: Let's say a church has one million dollars in its endowment, which earns an annual 8 percent. The goal for the first year is to use 4 percent of the earnings to fund tuition for selected individuals who meet established criteria. This method allows the other 4 percent of the endowment's earnings to grow while still enabling the church to fund $40,000 in tuition.

The endowment will pour out more funds in each subsequent year due to the compounding interest; therefore, the endowment will not go down unless there's a major shock to the stock markets. Endowments can be powerful tools for any church, but they should not be considered until all necessary initiatives are already funded.

REFERENCES

Carnegie, Dale. 1936. *How to Win Friends and Influence People.* New
    York: Gallery Books, a Division of Simon & Schuster, Inc.

Hagin, Kenneth E. 2001. *The Believer's Authority.* Tulsa: Faith Library
    Publications.

Harris, Alex and Brett. 2008. *Do Hard Things: A Teenage Rebellion.*
    Colorado Springs: Multnomah Books.

Leman, Dr. Kevin and Bill Pentak. 2004. *The Way of the Shepherd.*
    Grand Rapids: Zondervan.

McChesney, Chris, Sean Covey, and Jim Huling. 2021. *The 4
    Disciplines of Execution.* New York: Simon & Schuster.

Miller, Donald. 2017. *Building a Story Brand.* New York: Harper
    Collins Publishers.

Wickman, Gino. 2016. *Traction: Get a Grip on Your Business.* Dallas:
    BenBella Books, Inc.

James Boyd is a successful entrepreneur, pastor, church-health consultant, and author. He entered the business world immediately after graduating from high school, jumping with both feet into the auto industry, where for the next nine years he was literally sent around the world designing vehicles for major automakers.

Recognized as a prodigy in the industry, James simultaneously earned his Bachelor of Science degree in Design Engineering while building effective teams of people that worked for him in Japan, California, Michigan, and other parts of the Midwest United States.

Though a success by business standards, James experienced a continual sense of emptiness that all the money, connections, fame, and influence he was growing accustomed to could not fill. That's when he made the decision to move from Los Angeles back to his home state of Michigan to seek his purpose outside the successful life he'd built for himself.

James began serving at his local church and attended its Bible school, where the Word of God dispelled the sense of emptiness that he'd experienced for nearly a decade. But he soon experienced something new as well, and that something was a call to ministry.

James Boyd now holds both a bachelor's degree and a master's degree in theology from Life Christian University and has helped numerous churches in their pursuit of bringing health and a systematic approach to ministry. He owns multiple businesses that allow him to stay sharp in the business world and church world at the same time. His life experiences and background in business are an asset to pastors and ministry leaders who did not receive this essential training.

James and his wife, Tracy, serve as the lead pastors at Grow Church in Naples, Florida, and are the parents of three amazing adult daughters.

———————